8916

SAFE SCHOOLS

A Planning Guide
for Action

1995 Edition

Publishing Information

Safe Schools: A Planning Guide for Action (1995 Edition) was developed jointly by the California Department of Education and the Crime and Violence Prevention Center of the Office of the California Attorney General. The names of those involved in the development of the document appear in the acknowledgments.

This publication was edited by Sheila Bruton, working in cooperation with Carol Abbott, Consultant, School Safety and Violence Prevention Office, California Department of Education. It was designed and prepared for photo-offset production by the staff of CDE Press, with the cover and interior design created and prepared by Paul Lee. Typesetting was done by Carey Johnson.

Photographs were taken by Don Yee.

This document was published by the Department of Education, 721 Capitol Mall, Sacramento, California (mailing address: P.O. Box 944272, Sacramento, CA 94244-2720). It was printed by the Office of State Printing and distributed under the provisions of the Library Distribution Act and *Government Code* Section 11096.

ISBN 0-8011-0799-7
ISBN 0-8011-1191-9

Ordering Information

Copies of this publication are available for $10.75 each, plus sales tax for California residents, from the California Department of Education, CDE Press, Sales Unit, P.O. Box 271, Sacramento, CA 95812-0271; FAX (916) 323-0823. See page 150 for complete information on payment, including credit card purchases. Prices on all publications are subject to change.

A partial list of other educational resources available from the Department appears on page 149. In addition, the *1995 Educational Resources Catalog* describing publications, videos, and other instructional media available from the Department can be obtained without charge by writing to the address given above or by calling the Sales Unit at (916) 445-1260.

Notice

The guidance in *Safe Schools: A Planning Guide for Action* (1995 Edition) is not binding on local educational agencies or other entities. Except for the statutes, regulations, and court decisions that are referenced herein, the *Guide* is exemplary, and compliance with it is not mandatory. (See *Education Code* Section 33308.5.)

The statutes cited in this publication are current through September 1994.

Prepared for publication
by CSEA members.

Contents

Chapter 1: The Safe School Challenge

This chapter examines the detrimental influence of crime on school campuses and emphasizes the need for collaborative planning for safe schools. Legal, ethical, and educational rationales supporting the importance of safe school planning are presented. The proposal is made that a blending of the goals for safe schools and other school improvement efforts provides the most effective basis for successful safe school planning.

Chapter 2: The Safe School Model

This chapter provides the reader with an understanding of the factors affecting school safety. The recommended safe school model, consisting of four interacting components, is described in detail. The chapter outlines the effect of the four components on the overall school environment and ways in which the components interrelate with other school improvement efforts.

Chapter 3: Planning for Safe Schools

This chapter presents procedures for developing and implementing a written plan for a safe school. It offers suggestions for forming and motivating a broad-based committee and presents the skills, methods, and steps needed to implement a comprehensive, collaborative planning process. A discussion is included on how to use existing data sources in planning and evaluation.

Chapter 4: Safe School Strategies and Actions **43**

This chapter presents possible actions and strategies for prevention and intervention programs and restructuring efforts keyed to each of the four safe school components. The need is stressed for an individualized action plan prepared by the school safety committee.

Appendixes **65**

The appendixes provide further technical information needed to develop a safe school plan.

Selected Resources **145**

Preface

SINCE the first edition of *Safe Schools: A Planning Guide for Action* was published in 1989, community and school violence have exploded into the public spotlight. Parents are alarmed by the increase in violence and the threat that poses to their children. They are particularly worried about the rise in random youth violence spilling into their neighborhoods and schools. Many parents worry that the schools their children attend may no longer be safe and their communities no longer peaceful.

Young people are also worried about violence and its most ominous manifestation, the youth gun culture. In the document titled *Survey of Experiences, Perceptions, and Apprehensions About Guns Among Young People in America,* prepared for the Harvard School of Public Health, the researchers found that one serious consequence of the youth gun culture was that more than one in three young people in this country have concluded that their "chances of living to a ripe old age are likely to be cut short because of the threat of my being wiped out from guns."

Violence and guns are the more serious dimensions of school safety. We must also consider gangs, vandalism, theft, truancy, dropouts, and drug and alcohol abuse. Most important, we must be proactive, not reactive.

For these reasons and because of changes in the field of school safety, the California Department of Education and the Office of the California Attorney General, through the School/Law Enforce-

ment Partnership, are releasing this second edition of *Safe Schools: A Planning Guide for Action.* The guide shows schools how to form partnerships with law enforcement agencies and the community to develop a comprehensive safe school plan that includes the whole school environment. This guide should be used in conjunction with the Office of the California Attorney General's publication *Law in the School*, which provides a comprehensive look at statutory and case law relating to schools and their surrounding communities.

The School/Law Enforcement Partnership was formed in 1983 by the California Department of Education and the Office of the California Attorney General. The mission of the partnership is to provide leadership in promoting safe schools through interagency collaboration. In 1985 the Interagency School Safety Demonstration Act (Ch. 1457, Stats. 1985) formally established the partnership in law, requiring the partnership to sponsor school safety conferences, fund safe schools grants, and provide technical assistance to schools through a professional cadre.

Each year since 1990 the School/Law Enforcement Partnership has conducted 20 regional safe school planning workshops, demonstrating the planning strategies laid out in this guide. During the same period the partnership has distributed more than $2 million in grants to several hundred schools for implementing safe school plans.

The main purpose of California's schools is to educate children and provide them with the opportunity to participate fully in society as adults. But for education to be successful, we must provide safe and secure community and school environments in which children can learn and teachers can teach. By following the strategies and procedures for developing and implementing a written plan for safe schools, as recommended in this guide, schools can take positive steps to reach that goal.

JANE IRVINE HENDERSON
Deputy Superintendent
Children, Youth, and Family
Services Branch

MARY TOBIAS WEAVER
Program Administrator
School Safety and Violence
Prevention Office

M. DAVID STIRLING
Chief Deputy Attorney General
Office of the California Attorney General

CAROLYN ORTIZ
Director
Crime and Violence Prevention Center
Office of the California Attorney General

Acknowledgments

THE California Department of Education and the Office of the California Attorney General wish to thank the many people who have made this publication possible. First, thanks are extended again to the many individuals who were involved in developing the first edition.

Special thanks are due to the following persons for this second edition: **Mike Barta,** Desert Sands Unified School District; **John Burton,** Office of the San Bernardino County Superintendent of Schools; **Tad Kitada,** Placer County Office of Education; **Lee Lundberg,** San Leandro Unified School District; **Linda Winchester,** Office of the Sacramento County District Attorney; **Mary Tobias Weaver,** California Department of Education; **Steve Jefferies, Michael Jett,** and **Carolyn Ortiz,** Office of the California Attorney General.

Special thanks are also extended to the members of the School/Law Enforcement Partnership cadre who have trained hundreds of schools on safe school planning, using a curriculum adapted from the ideas contained in this guide.

Lastly, special appreciation is expressed to **Carol Abbott,** California Department of Education, for coordinating the revision team and editing this second edition of *Safe Schools: A Planning Guide for Action;* and to **Allan Keown,** Department of Education, for reviewing the document from a legal perspective.

Glossary of Codes and Abbreviations

The following codes are cited in the text:

CC	*Civil Code*
CCR	*California Code of Regulations*
EC	*Education Code*
FERPA	(Federal) Family Educational Rights to Privacy Act
GC	*Government Code*
H&SC	*Health and Safety Code* (California)
PC	*Penal Code*
USC	*United States Code*
VC	*Vehicle Code*
W&IC	*Welfare and Institutions Code*

The following abbreviations are used in the text:

ESL	English as a second language
DATE	Drug, alcohol, and tobacco education
HKHC	Healthy Kids, Healthy California programs
IEP	Individualized Educational Program
PQR	Program quality review (teams review school programs for effectiveness)
SARB	School Attendance Review Board
SED	Severely emotionally disturbed
SIP	School Improvement Program
WASC	Western Association of Schools and Colleges (reviews for accreditation)

Introduction

SAFE *Schools: A Planning Guide for Action* presents the latest ideas about creating safe school environments. The recommendations come from successful education and law enforcement partners who have tested the strategies in communities as large as Los Angeles and as small as Joshua Tree. In short, the safe schools process works. It has been refined and revised over the past ten years and now represents the wisdom and experience of hundreds of dedicated professionals.

The core of that wisdom can be expressed in four basic principles.

First, safe schools are caring schools. Students in safe schools feel respected and know that the people in that learning community care about their individual needs and expect them to succeed. The students' cultural heritage is respected, and there is tolerance for racial, language, physical, and ethnic differences in the school. Similarly, staff members in a safe school perceive that they are safe and that their ideas about school improvement are valued. Safe schools welcome parents and community members who share their ideas, talents, and resources in improving the school environment and make the school a valued part of the community.

Second, safe schools are built through the cooperative efforts of parents, students, teachers, security staff, classified staff, law enforcement representatives, and community members. The continued involvement of a broad spectrum of the community in the design and

constant revision of a safe school plan ensures that the community stays informed and invested in the endeavor to keep the school a safe and successful learning community. The community's involvement also ensures that there are alternatives in the community to assist students who have difficulties adjusting to the school environment.

Third, safe schools communicate high standards. Students and staff know that learning and achievement are encouraged and highly valued and that positive social behaviors are expected. They know that the achievement of each individual is valued regardless of innate academic or physical talents. The consequences for violating the rules and standards are equally clear.

Fourth, safe schools stress *prevention,* and the staff and students are *prepared.* Ongoing training opportunities allow students and staff to increase their ability to deal with conflict, anger, and other threats to safety. Safe schools have security checks on a regular basis to identify potential physical hazards or the school's vulnerability to crime and vandalism. They also institute ongoing programs to prevent gang activity; drug, tobacco, and alcohol abuse; and other negative behaviors. Finally, because it is impossible to prevent all problems, safe schools have crisis response plans in place to deal with unforeseen emergencies.

This manual examines the issue of safety in schools and recommends strategies and actions for adoption by safe school teams or committees as part of a comprehensive safe school plan. Chapter

1 discusses the challenge of providing school safety—a challenge that requires communities to balance the civil rights of individuals with the majority's right to safety. Chapter 2 describes a safe school model organized under four broad components: the personal characteristics of students and staff; the school's physical environment; the school's social environment; and the school's culture. Chapter 3 recommends a seven-step planning process to guide the school committee in addressing the components of the safe school model. The steps are as follows: identify your safe school planning committee members; create a vision for your school; gather and analyze information about your school and its community; identify your school's and community's areas of desired change; set your major goal(s); select and implement strategies for each safe school component; and evaluate and assess your progress. Chapter 4 suggests practical strategies and actions for achieving safety in each of the four components.

The appendixes contain references to the *Education Code,* the *Government Code,* and other resources. In addition, many forms are included that will prove invaluable to school planning committee members as they gather data about their school and its perceived safety and develop goals and strategies for action.

If a school committee follows the steps and components of a safe school plan that are outlined in this manual, the committee can be reasonably sure that all aspects of safety have been considered. In the past physical security measures were the preferred way of addressing safety. However, experience shows that the social, economic, and cultural forces now present in the community make a more comprehensive strategy imperative. To be successful in protecting students and staff from physical harm while caring for their emotional health and safety, schools must look at developing a comprehensive plan that addresses all the components and steps described in this manual.

This document is a joint effort of the State Superintendent of Public Instruction and the Attorney General through the School/Law Enforcement Partnership. The partnership provides a cadre of law enforcement and education professionals who are experienced and trained in helping schools adapt this process to develop a safe school plan. The cadre's services are free to schools through legislation that established the partnership in 1984. The partnership is jointly administered by the California Department of Education and the Attorney General's Crime and Violence Prevention Center.

A list of the cadre's services is included in Appendix J. Questions about school safety, the partnership, the cadre, or workshops for designing a safe school plan can be addressed to either of the following agencies:

School Safety and Violence
    Prevention Office
California Department of Education
P.O. Box 944272
Sacramento, CA 94244-2720
(916) 657-2989
FAX: (916) 657-5263

Crime and Violence Prevention Center
Office of the California Attorney General
P.O. Box 944255
Sacramento, CA 94244-2550
(916) 324-7863
FAX: (916) 327-2384

Chapter 1

The Safe School Challenge

Violence in Schools

The terrifying thing is that the nature of
school crimes has grown more violent,
[and] the perpetrators steadily younger.
A University of Michigan study reports
that 9 percent of eighth graders carry a
gun, knife, or club to school at least once
a month. In all, an estimated 270,000
guns go to school every day. . . . Twenty
percent of the suburban high schoolers
surveyed by Tulane researchers Joseph
Sheley and M. Dwayne Smith endorsed
shooting someone "who has stolen something from you." Concluded the researchers: "One is struck less by the armament
[among today's teenagers] than by the
evident willingness to pull the trigger."

—U.S. News & World Report,
November 8, 1993

S AFE schools are increasingly difficult to achieve as crime and violence grow in the communities of California. Concerns about school safety are real. Consider the following grim statistics:

- The FBI's Violent Crimes Index indicates that between 1987 and 1991 the number of arrests of juveniles increased by 50 percent—twice the increase for persons eighteen years of age or older. Most alarming, juvenile arrests for murder during the same period increased by 85 percent. (Arrests for persons aged eighteen years and older increased 21 percent.) In 1982 arrests of teenagers thirteen to fifteen years of age for murder numbered 390; a decade later that figure had jumped to 740.
- According to *U.S. News & World Report* (November 8, 1993), more than three million crimes a year are committed in or near the 85,000 public schools in the United States.
- In a 1991 report the U.S. Centers for Disease Control and Prevention indicated that one in 20 students will bring a gun to school at least once a month.
- *The National Education Goals Report* (1992) reported that 16 percent of the nation's twelfth graders admitted they had received violent threats and that half of those youths sustained injuries in school.

- The 1993 *USA Weekend* survey of 65,000 youths revealed that 55 percent of the students in grades ten through twelve know that weapons are regularly brought to school; 79 percent said that violence often occurs from "stupid things, like bumping into someone."
- *U.S. News & World Report* (January 17, 1994) notes: "For many years the violent-crime rate seemed to rise and fall in tandem with the number of teens in the population. But teen violence exploded—murder arrests of youths under eighteen have jumped 92 percent since 1985—during a period when the teen population remained steady or declined. A projected 23 percent increase by 2005 in youths ages fifteen to nineteen may make things worse."

Experts from all levels of government acknowledge that schools are not the source of the violence. Community violence spills into the schools.

What Is a Safe School?

Safe schools are orderly and purposeful places in which students and staff are free to learn and teach without the threat of physical and psychological harm. Such schools have developed a strong sense of community. A visitor to the campus will see signs of student affiliation and bonding to the school and sensitivity and respect for all persons, including those of other cultural and ethnic backgrounds. Safe schools provide an environment of nonviolence, set clear behavioral expectations, institute disciplinary policies that are consistently and fairly administered, and accord recognition for positive behavior. Safe schools have established policies for proactive security procedures, emergency response plans, and the timely maintenance, cleanliness, and attractive appearance of the campus and classrooms.

Who Is Responsible for School Safety?

Society is relying increasingly on schools to address pressing social issues. But developing solutions to social problems that affect school safety requires expertise not generally possessed by educators. Although educators have the primary role in developing comprehensive school-site safety plans, they cannot shoulder that responsibility alone. For example, students who have difficulty adjusting to the school environment may benefit from mental health services or alternate placements. Now, more than ever, there is a need to work with community and law enforcement agencies in a concerted team effort to improve the safety of California's public schools.

What Are the Reasons for Safety Planning?

Students and the social concerns and stresses that they bring to school have changed dramatically over the years. Poverty, the changing family structure, drugs, racial and cultural tensions, media influences, and other social stresses—in short, all community problems—have an impact on schools and affect the learning envi-

A Safe School Is . . .

- A happy school for kids, so kids don't get hurt by bullies. *(Christopher, grade one)*
- Where there are no knives or guns, no punching or kicking, no beating up people, no painting on the walls. *(Brent, grade two)*
- A safe community and has fire equipment and also has safe friends . . . who don't do drugs. A safe community is an area where you can go out and play without an adult because you can trust people around the area. *(Chris, grade four)*
- A school that has nothing that can harm you or anybody else. A safe school is a place where you can go with your friends and not be bothered by any strangers. A safe school is a place where you can learn well and get a good education. *(Cyzana, grade six)*

—Students, Ellen Feickert Elementary School, Elk Grove, California

ronment to some degree. In the face of these stresses, schools have four main reasons to provide safe schooling to all students. The reasons are educational, legal, social, and fiscal.

First and foremost there is an *educational* reason for safe school planning. Schools are created to provide an optimum learning environment that allows teachers to effectively teach and students to actively learn. Providing such an environment is a fundamental responsibility of each school employee, whether certificated or classified. Crime and violence occurring on or around a school campus significantly interfere with providing such an environment. Effective teaching, regardless of how inspired, and meaningful learning, regardless of how eagerly it is sought, cannot truly take root and flourish in a school that fails to provide for the

We Are *All* Responsible

Each of us can make a difference, no matter whether we are the Attorney General or a senior at Eastern High. If we care about others, if we say we are sick and fed up with violence and we want to do something for our school, our family, and our community, nobody is out of the picture. Everybody can be involved and make a difference, and by joining together everyone concerned, I think we can put an end to violence. But it needs you. You are the strength of America, you are the future.

—*U.S. Attorney General Janet Reno, in an address to Eastern Senior High School, Washington, D.C., November 17, 1993*

physical, emotional, and psychological safety and well-being of its students and staff. The process of safe school planning allows a school and its community to be both effective and proactive as they cooperatively identify and root out impediments to the business of learning.

Another important reason for safe school planning is the *legal* responsibility of schools to provide equal education for all students. When students are frightened to attend school or are preoccupied with their safety while in class, they are being denied their right to education as envisioned by the architects of public education. Furthermore, equal access to quality education is not provided to students who must attend schools located in high-crime communities and, as a result, suffer from more serious safety concerns than do students who attend schools in relatively low-crime neighborhoods.

A third reason for safe school planning relates to the *social* responsibility of schools. Every future drug user, suicide victim, gang member, dropout, child abuse victim, and arsonist is probably at one time a student. Thus schools are unique because they are the only entity in society that can positively affect every student in the nation, despite potentially negative social influences on the student. By addressing the four components and seven steps of safe school planning, schools can develop programs that resolve negative conditions and give every student a chance to reach his or her full potential.

A final reason for safe school planning is becoming more apparent during this time of reduced budgets and increased violence. Because resources have diminished, schools have a *financial re-*

sponsibility to taxpayers to ensure that the money brings maximum benefit to both school safety and the learning enterprise. Preventing youth violence ensures that a majority of resources goes to the classroom instead of to such things as graffiti removal and vandalism repairs. A safe school builds public confidence in education.

There is also a *financial benefit* to safe school planning. The process of conducting a needs assessment and building a community-school team may enable a school to qualify for outside grant funds and resources, such as safety credits. Safety credits are available through self-insurance pools and allow schools to set aside funds for enhancing employee safety. These seldom-used credits can be used to purchase disaster supplies and to provide staff training on safety issues.

Comprehensive planning for youth-violence prevention and safe schools is essential if schools and communities are to confront the issues that interfere with learning, the operation of the school, and the general health of the community. Safe school planning is essential not only for the welfare of society but also for schools to retain the public trust in their responsibility for providing quality education to all students in a cost-effective manner.

How Do Changing Relationships Affect Safety?

The regulatory books are full of laws on safe schools and closed campuses. Yet schools cannot keep outsiders off campuses, and school violence is at an all-time high. Laws alone are inadequate for addressing the problem.

At its core the challenge to provide safe schools is a *people problem*. Chang-

"They Don't Know . . ."

I don't feel safe in school because teachers and administrators can't always know what's going on. They don't know or see everything that we as students see. There is so much violence at school because kids aren't taught or are not learning respect, consideration, or discipline. They know they can get away with almost anything. Some kids are just uncontrollable.

—Bernadette, age sixteen, quoted in LA Youth, The Newspaper by and About Los Angeles Teens, *November-December, 1993*

ing relationships are often the source of liability or morale problems for schools because many adults base their decisions on folklore: they assume that schools still operate as they did in the past and that the rules governing student-adult relationships are unchanged. The reality is that changing case law and emerging legal trends are redefining the distinctive relationships within the schools. Therefore, circumstances require that schools take a new look at the relationships they build among students, staff, and the community at every stage of planning and intervention. To establish safe schools, schools must dispel folklore, acknowledge current realities, and achieve a balance between the rights of individuals and the need to ensure order and safety on campus. To achieve such a balance, schools should consider the following issues affecting relationships in the schools.

First, the compulsory education laws create a *special relationship* between students and staff. Students in California are compelled to attend school from the time they are six years old until they are eighteen years old, and the parents are required to send their children to school. In addition, students have a constitutional guarantee to a safe and secure environment for learning. If a school fails to acknowledge unsafe conditions, then its staff has not guaranteed a safe environment—and students are not free to flee or leave. With knowledge of safe school planning, schools can create positive learning environments that are free from hazards and fear.

The second issue, closely related to the first, is that decisions and policies on safe schools cannot ignore the *civil rights* of students and staff members. For example, the rights of students under the First Amendment to the U.S. Constitution must be considered when developing dress codes or policies dealing with underground newspapers and under the Fourth Amendment when establishing policies governing searches of students and their property by school staff members. In addition, staff members and students injured on campus have effectively used the federal Civil Rights Act, Section 1983, along with the Fourteenth Amendment of the U.S. Constitution, when challenging school districts about the safety of the schools. Therefore, staff should be familiar with civil rights provisions and with court decisions indicating new interpretations of civil rights. Inherent in this discussion is the understanding that a safe school plan needs to balance the rights of the majority with the rights of the individual.

Third, the school has a *duty to protect*. The school is responsible for providing adequate supervision on campus. The creation of rules, policies, and procedures does not alone exempt the staff or district from legal action by people injured on campuses because students are still mi-

Opportunities to Develop Self-Respect

I think that the problems of delinquency—drugs, youth gangs, teen pregnancy, and youth violence—are symptoms of a deeper problem in society. For too long we have forgotten and neglected our children, and there is no one specific delinquency prevention effort that can make a difference. . . . We must encourage our children to take part in public and community service. So many children join gangs in order to belong and to participate. Let's organize efforts that attract our young people and give them an opportunity to serve this nation and to develop a feeling of self-respect through constructive activity.

—*U.S. Attorney General Janet Reno,*
quoted in Juvenile Justice, *Fall/Winter, 1993*

nors. Society has not awarded them recognition for mature judgment. They are prohibited from buying alcohol, and very few are allowed to vote or be licensed to drive an automobile. Therefore, schools must constantly be alert to their duties to provide for safety through adequate supervision.

The final consideration affecting relationships, *acting under the color of authority,* involves situations in which school staff command students to follow orders given by an authority figure. Recent court decisions show that despite student compliance, rules given under a display of authority may not withstand legal action. Although acting under the color of authority is often expedient, the term implies the adult's responsibility to act legally and fairly and to show respect for students. For example, if an adult displaying authority makes an unreasonable demand on a student or deprives the student of his or her civil rights (such as a First Amendment right relating to a dress code), the student might challenge that authority by seeking legal recourse. The school might then find that it is open to serious liability or to reversal of its decisions. Students might also rebel against what they see as an unreasonable display of authority. That situation leads to further morale and disciplinary problems.

Schools, then, face the challenge of creating "safe, secure, and peaceful" campuses while reflecting the democratic principles of exercising personal and social responsibility and respecting the rights of individuals. Creating safe schools is a part of the educational process. It is incumbent on schools to teach students how to function peacefully. If schools develop safe and secure environments at the expense of democratic values, they have lost sight of their educational mission.

Law in the School

Goal 7: Safe, Disciplined, and Alcohol- and Drug-Free Schools

(A) By the year 2000 every school in the United States will be free of drugs, violence, and the unauthorized presence of firearms and alcohol and will offer a disciplined environment conducive to learning.

(B) The objectives for this goal are that—

  (i) Every school will implement a firm and fair policy on use, possession, and distribution of drugs and alcohol;

  (ii) Parents, businesses, governmental and community organizations will work together to ensure the rights of students to study in a safe and secure environment that is free of drugs and crime, and that schools provide a healthy environment and are a safe haven for all children;

  (iii) Every local educational agency will develop and implement a policy to ensure that all schools are free of violence and the unauthorized presence of weapons;

  (iv) Every local educational agency will develop a sequential, comprehensive kindergarten through twelfth grade drug and alcohol prevention education program;

  (v) Drug and alcohol curriculum should be taught as an integral part of sequential, comprehensive health education;

  (vi) Community-based teams should be organized to provide students and teachers with needed support; and

  (vii) Every school should work to eliminate sexual harassment.

—*Public Law 103-227 (March 31, 1994),*
§102, 108 Stat. 130

Chapter 2

The Safe School Model

Links Among Schools, Communities, and Families

If we are to overcome violence and the fear that accompanies that violence, we must remember that prevention is the real long-term cure. Our greatest challenge may be to follow up our first response to an incident, which often is to increase security measures, with other strategies designed to address complex, systemwide problems. We must involve parents and community members in innovative ways. And we **must** involve students themselves and invite them to join in developing long-term solutions, such as peer counseling and conflict resolution. Schools are only as safe as the communities in which they are located.

—Delaine Eastin
State Superintendent of
Public Instruction

PLANNING for safe schools should not duplicate the process of other school improvement efforts. Instead, safe school planning should be one aspect of a comprehensive plan for an effective school. The planning team should incorporate safety plans in the planning and evaluation processes already established in the school.

Drug, alcohol, and tobacco prevention plans, school discipline rules, restructuring plans, crisis response plans, dropout prevention programs, and school safety plans all belong in an integrated school improvement process. When the school incorporates school safety into the ongoing school planning efforts, there will be regular review and update of the entire process and a minimum amount of duplication. (See Appendix B for the correlation between safe school planning, the curriculum frameworks, and grade-span reform initiatives; and Appendix I for *Education Code* Sections 35294, 35294.1, and 35294.5, which relate to safe school plans.)

Research indicates that a comprehensive approach to creating safe and effective schools must include four components that interact and affect the safety of the whole campus. The four components are the personal characteristics of students and staff, the school's physical environment, the school's social environment, and the school's culture. These four components form the basis for developing a safe school model as outlined in this publication.

Component 1

Personal Characteristics of Students and Staff

It is difficult, if not impossible, to create a safe school plan without a clear knowledge of the people—students and staff—who will mingle at that school every day. Personal characteristics that should be considered include the ethnic and cultural backgrounds and expectations, health concerns, life experiences, and unique qualities that students and staff bring to the school. These characteristics reflect the social and economic conditions of the community and affect the school in many ways. Although schools cannot modify anyone's personal characteristics and past life experiences, schools can have a strong influence on the current experiences of students and staff by implementing school safety planning and actions.

Healing the Wounds

Violence directed at individuals because of their physical or cultural characteristics or beliefs is intolerable in this or any other society. The public schools—with the cooperation and assistance of parents, students, business and community representatives—have the moral obligation to prevent, combat, and heal the wounds from hate violence through curriculum and instruction, student support services and activities, and, when necessary, direct intervention.

—California State Board of Education Policy on Hate-Motivated Violence

Three major objectives of safe school planning are to (1) gain insight into and understand the ways which existing personal characteristics affect a school's physical, social, and cultural environments; (2) determine how the school can positively affect those environments; and (3) develop an attitude of acceptance and mutual respect among *all* students and staff for the unique attributes that they bring with them. See Table 1 at the end of this chapter for a summary of the goals for this component.

Component 2

The School's Physical Environment

The school's physical environment can strongly affect the students' and the

community's perceptions of the safety of that school. Therefore, addressing the physical environment is often the most traditional school safety practice. Security practices include installing required public signs, appropriate lighting, fencing, and alarms. In conjunction with security practices, the school's location and appearance have a dramatic effect on whether the school is perceived as safe. The maintenance of the school's grounds, buildings, and classrooms affects—positively or negatively—the public's perception of the comfort and safety of the students, staff, and community.

Many of the physical features of the school cannot be altered, and the school will have to take those features into account in developing safety policies and procedures. Effective security procedures and the timely maintenance, cleanliness, and appearance of the grounds, buildings, and classrooms require planning and action and will bring significant rewards in school safety and the perception of

Importance of Early Intervention

These findings highlight the need for early intervention to help children conquer their environment. Researchers have found that kids as young as seven can learn to heal themselves by telling stories about the violence they have suffered. And some experts think older kids can be turned away from crime when they are forced to confront directly what violence does to others.

—U.S. News & World Report, January 17, 1994

They Need Adults Who Care

Students desire authentic relationships in which they are trusted, given responsibility, spoken to honestly and warmly, and treated with dignity and respect. They feel adults inside schools are too busy, don't understand, or just don't care about them.

—Voices from the Inside

safety. The proper use of risk management techniques allows school personnel to recognize and evaluate physical hazards and activities that can cause injuries or property loss. The objective is to correct those situations and eliminate the risk, thus enabling the schools to save tremendous amounts of money and restore public confidence.

Any school can create an environment that is inviting and promotes safety, pride, sense of ownership, and freedom from fear. Such physical environments enhance the school climate and are an essential, interrelated component of safe schools. See Table 2 at the end of this chapter for a summary of planning goals for this component.

Component 3

The School's Social Environment

The school's organizational structure includes leadership styles, classroom management strategies, curricula, and the organization of daily activities. Each of these interactions is a powerful mechanism affecting the social environment and, therefore, school safety. Working toward safer and more effective schools demands an evaluation of how well the school has implemented shared decision making and how well the school's organizational structure reinforces safe practices, high standards, and mutual respect. Schools will need to evaluate whether

Risk Management

Every school district has an insurance carrier or, if self-funded, a third-party administrator. The risk management training and experience of those professionals should be used to produce a risk management plan for the district and for each school site. Staff trained in risk management should be designated at the district level as risk managers. They should be furnished on a regular basis with information about the amounts and types of claims received so that they know where to concentrate their attention. A local and state network of all those with risk management responsibility can be organized for training and the regular exchange of ideas. By planning ahead, schools can prevent losses, and children and staff can be protected from harm.

students understand and accept the rules and know that the staff will consistently enforce them. Staff members should ensure that they make every effort to recognize and reinforce desirable behavior.

A safe school plan will evaluate school practices that focus on preventing violence and building resiliency and the ways in which the school's programs foster the development of personal, social, and academic skills. The plan will ensure that curricula and staff development topics include self-esteem, self-identity, emotional development, anger management, student responsibility, social expectations, decision making, career decisions, goal setting, effective communication, and effective relationships.

Finally, the degree to which the principal, staff, students, parents, and, when appropriate, representatives from law enforcement agencies and the community are able to interact and participate in the decision-making processes of the school will have a fundamental effect on the school's safety. See Table 3 at the end of this chapter for a summary of goals for this component.

Component 4
The School's Culture

Perhaps the most accurate measure of the health of the school is the school's culture. It deals with intangibles and includes the implicit assumptions, expectations, and knowledge of students, parents, and staff about how the school should function and how individuals in school should act. The school's culture also includes the informal rules, norms, beliefs, and values that govern the daily behavior of students, staff, and administrators.

Conversation About Values

Our data suggest that parents, teachers, students, staff, and administrators of all ethnicities and classes value and desire education, honesty, integrity, beauty, care, justice, truth, courage, and meaningful hard work. . . . However, very little time is spent in classrooms discussing these issues, and a number of restrictions exist against doing so. In the beginning of our research, many participants initially assumed other participants held different values. The more we talked, the more this assumption was challenged. Students desire a network of adults (parents and teachers) with whom they can "really talk about important things," and they want to have these conversations about values with one another.

—Voices from the Inside

Focusing on the school's culture by developing a greater sense of affiliation and community among staff and students will help positively affect behavioral norms, such as the code of silence that inhibits students from alerting authorities to potentially dangerous situations on campus. A positive school culture exists when the school acts as a *community* in which high levels of respect, affiliation, and bonding develop among students and staff. In positive school communities members accept the established behavioral and academic expectations and goals. In addition, the curriculum meets the needs of students with differing learning styles. See Table 4 at the end of this chapter for a list of potential goals for this component.

Project YES! Gang Violence- and Drug-Prevention Curriculum

With a grant from the California Governor's Office of Criminal Justice Planning, the Orange County Office of Education developed Project YES! (Yes to Education and Skills) as part of its gang violence- and drug-prevention curriculum. To help bring prevention curriculum into the classroom, Lucky Stores, Inc., provides matching funds for any school or district in California to purchase the curriculum. Curriculum modules for grades two through seven are available, and lessons focus on the following themes: responsible citizenship, the dynamics of cultural diversity, choices and consequences, refusal skills, and success and achievement.

Enhancing Resiliency in Schools

Fostering resiliency isn't something we do *to* kids per se. Rather, protective-factor research has clearly shown us that the development of resiliency is the process of healthy human development that is based on and grows out of nurturing, participatory relationships grounded in trust and respect. If we as adults and preventionists are truly concerned with preventing problems like alcohol and other drug abuse, then it is imperative that we make our central vision and mission the creation of supportive relationships with youths and their families.

> —*Bonnie Benard, Western Regional Center for Drug-Free Schools and Communities, Far West Laboratory for Educational Research and Development*

What Is School Culture?

When you walk into a school, you may get a global impression of the school's distinctive tone or character. What cues lead to that impression? The walls and their decorations, the floors and the way they are polished, the demeanor of students and staff walking through the halls, the nature of the instruction that takes place in classrooms, the relationships between staff and administrators? Behind or beneath the cues . . . lies a shared set of organizing principles called culture.

> —*F. Erickson, "Conceptions of School Culture: An Overview,"* Educational Administration Quarterly, *Vol. 23 (November, 1987). Reprinted by permission of Sage Publications, Inc.*

Building Resiliency in Youth

Resilience can be defined as the capacity to spring back, rebound, successfully adapt in the face of adversity, and develop social competence, despite exposure to severe stress.

School Practices That Foster Resiliency

1. Caring and support:
   - Promote relationships with teachers.
   - Promote relationships with friends and peers.

2. High expectations:
   - Provide success for all students.
   - Promote social and scholastic success.
   - Foster high self-esteem.

3. Opportunities for participation and involvement:
   - Provide opportunities to participate.
   - Promote responsibilities for making decisions, planning, and helping others.
   - Promote engagement rather than alienation.

Source: *School/Community Violence Prevention: Focus on Gangs.* Sacramento: California Department of Education and the Office of the California Attorney General, 1994. Quoting from materials developed by the Western Center for Drug-Free Schools and Communities. (See Appendix C for more information about fostering resiliency in youths.)

Table 1

Personal Characteristics of Students and Staff

(The experiences of students, teachers, administrators, and other personnel in the school)

Safe School Subcomponent	Planning Goal
Ethnic/cultural diversity of students	The backgrounds of all students will be acknowledged, respected, and incorporated into the school curriculum and activities. Bilingual and English-as-a-second-language (ESL) programs will be provided; cultural integration efforts will be incorporated in orientations and guidance programs.
Life experiences of students and staff	Social-service support systems will be coordinated with schools to provide needed services (e.g., food, clothing, shelter, protective services, parenting classes, support groups). Curriculum and special programs will be designed and modified to address issues relevant to the student body (e.g., gangs, drugs, family structures). The unique talents and gifts of students and staff will be recognized, and efforts will be made to enable people to share those gifts and talents in school programs and committees.
Staff expertise/ diversity	Staff members with diversified expertise who represent, in proportion, the gender and racial or ethnic backgrounds of the students will be recruited to work effectively with students. Staff will receive ongoing in-service training to meet the changing needs of the student body (e.g., training in conflict resolution, anger management, cultural awareness, ESL, alcohol and other drug-use prevention, and child abuse reporting requirements).
Physical/health concerns	Educational programs will be geared to specific health issues (e.g., nutrition, alcohol and other drug-use prevention). Schools will coordinate with community health services for prevention and intervention programs for students and their families. Schools will coordinate with mental health and alternative placement programs to ensure that severely emotionally disturbed (SED) students, or others who have difficulty adjusting to the school environment, receive appropriate educational services.

Table 2   17

Table 2
The School's Physical Environment
(The physical setting and conditions of the school)

Safe School Subcomponent	Planning Goal
School location	The school, whether or not in close proximity to businesses and commercial centers, will be an integral part of the community through its role in interagency efforts and community activities. The school will seek the cooperation of nearby businesses to obtain information on possible student crimes and truancy. (Such cooperation discourages crime near school campuses—crimes that may affect the safety of persons on the school campus.) The school will be alert to exposure to safety hazards, such as toxins or heavy traffic, from nearby commercial areas.
School grounds	The campus perimeter will be secure from criminal activity. The campus will be closed to outsiders, and access signs will be displayed prominently at entry points (PC §§ 627.2, 627.6, and EC § 32211[e]). Vehicles will not have easy access to school grounds. Places for loitering will be limited; bathrooms will be patrolled; lockers will be visible for supervision; and appropriate lighting will be installed in hallways. Physical conditions that could lead to accidental harm (e.g., damaged fences or lights, broken glass) will be corrected promptly. When rehabilitating, relocating, or remodeling, schools will consider environmental design concepts that foster adequate supervision and promote physical safety. The school will have adequate fencing for swimming pools, proper protection against slipping in hallways and stairwells, adequate protection against falls from recreational equipment, and landscape designs that prevent students from climbing to dangerous heights. The school policy for dealing with vandalism will include procedures for painting over graffiti before students arrive on campus and for replacing broken windows immediately.
School buildings and classrooms	School buildings and classrooms will be well maintained and attractive, free of physical hazards, and designed to prevent criminal activities.

Table 2 *(Continued)*

Safe School Subcomponent	Planning Goal
School buildings and classrooms	Classrooms will have an appropriate amount of space for the student-teacher ratio and will be decorated in an interesting manner.
Internal security procedures	Standard incident-reporting procedures will be in place. Valuables and equipment will be inventoried properly, engraved for identification, and stored securely. Campus security personnel will receive appropriate training (e.g., on days when teachers are receiving staff development activities under Senate Bill 1882), coordinated with law enforcement agencies. Parents and volunteers will be recruited and trained as monitors. The community will use the school during off-hours. The school and community will collaborate on crime prevention efforts. A crisis response plan will identify procedures to follow during (1) human emergencies, such as bomb threats, death of a student, suicide pacts, weapons on campus, and riots; and (2) natural emergencies, such as fires, earthquakes, and other natural disasters. School or district risk managers will consider applying for safety credits through their self-insurance pool to help finance employee safety measures, purchase disaster supplies, or provide staff training on safety issues.

Table 3   19

Table 3
The School's Social Environment
(The leadership and organizational processes of the school)

Safe School Subcomponent	Planning Goal
Leadership	The principal will provide strong leadership and a vision for school achievement, establish a positive style and tone, and set the direction for the school.
	The principal will facilitate shared decision making, involving the certificated and noncertificated staff, school police or security personnel, students, parents, and community members—particularly those members representing law enforcement and social service agencies.
	The principal will emphasize the importance of positive staff attitudes toward and treatment of students and parents; the principal will model and expect the staff to demonstrate responsiveness, respect, consideration, and sensitivity.
	The principal will be readily available to all members of the school community and will be highly visible on the campus and in classrooms.
	The principal will be actively involved in curricular matters and in establishing teams.
School-site management	Students, parents, certificated and classified staff, and, where appropriate, representatives from the community, law enforcement agencies, and businesses will participate in goal-setting decision making at the school level.
	Parents and representatives from businesses and law enforcement and community agencies will be actively engaged in the planning process for the school, whenever appropriate.
	A plan for the support of students, parents, and staff will be developed in a collaborative manner with representatives from law enforcement agencies, the community, private businesses, and the health professions.
	Services will be available to meet the needs of students and families.
Classroom organization and structure	Classroom conditions will provide an orderly learning environment, enhance the experience of learning, and promote positive interactions among students and staff.

Table 3 *(Continued)*

Safe School Subcomponent	*Planning Goal*
Classroom organization and structure	**C**urricula focusing on prevention will be developed to foster personal and social skills development. Topics will include responsible citizenship, appreciation of cultural diversity, choices, refusal skills, self-esteem, self-identity, emotional development, anger management, student responsibility, social expectations, decision making, career decisions, goal setting, effective communication, and effective relationships.

Learning styles of students will be routinely assessed, and appropriate instructional strategies will be used to accommodate the varying styles that students bring to the classroom.

Grouping and tracking by ability will be used sparingly and only for clearly defined educational objectives.

Instructional time will be maximized; disruptions will be minimized.

Students will be encouraged to work together on academic tasks through cooperative learning.

Building positive relationships will be a schoolwide theme.

Curricula will be designed to meet the diverse learning styles of students.

Strategies and programs will be implemented to ensure that students are not permitted or able to victimize more vulnerable students. |
| Discipline and consequences | **C**onsequences for violating behavioral and academic expectations will be fair and will be disseminated to and understood by students and staff.

Staff members will respond fairly and consistently to violations, including disciplinary issues and criminal infractions.

Policies and procedures will be established for reporting all criminal behavior on the school campus to the appropriate law enforcement agency.

Disciplinary practices will be developed with the active participation of all certificated and noncertificated staff; will involve students in problem-solving situations; and will focus on the cause of the problems, not the symptoms.

Discipline will be a developmental process aimed at changes in behavior and attitude and will not be merely a punitive reaction. |
| Participation and involvement | **P**artnerships will be purposely facilitated; students, parents, teachers, and community members will be involved in curriculum planning, training workshops, and other safe school planning and activities. |

Table 3   21

Table 3 *(Continued)*

Safe School Subcomponent	Planning Goal
Participation and involvement	**P**olice and fire representatives and district or county risk managers will participate in safety reviews of the campus, make presentations to students and staff, and assist staff to respond more effectively to school security and safety crises. A similar team might help in the design of new schools. **A** multidisciplinary approach will be encouraged; community support agencies, such as mental health, child protective services, and juvenile probation, will take an active part in school matters. **P**arents will be involved in decision making and policy formation; the home-school relationship will be positive. **S**tudents, staff, and parents will have a strong sense that what happens to the school is "my" concern. **P**arks and recreation department representatives will participate in planning and will cooperate with the school in providing after-school recreation programs.

Table 4: The School's Culture

(The general atmosphere or spirit of the school)

Safe School Subcomponent	Planning Goal
Affiliation and bonding	Students and staff will feel physically and psychologically secure from physical and verbal attacks.
	Students, parents, and staff will work together to ensure that strategies are in place to build a sense of community within the school so that all can feel pride in their school and feel that they are important members of a team.
	The dignity and heritage of each person will be affirmed and respected.
	Strategies will be implemented to break the code of silence among students and enable students to take ownership of plans for the safety of all by reporting weapons on campus or other threats to the health and welfare of all persons at school.
	Students and staff will be concerned about what happens to each other.
	Students and staff will accept ownership of conditions and events that happen at school.
	Students and staff will work together with a minimum of favoritism.
Behavioral expectations	Expectations will be clearly stated and known to everyone.
	Adults will model respectful, positive behaviors when dealing with students.
	The entire school community will participate in developing behavioral expectations.
	The school will model high moral standards, send positive messages to students, and show that the school and community expect the best effort and performance from everyone.
Academic expectations	Learning and productivity will be valued, and success will be expected of everyone.
	Clear and positive academic expectations will be communicated to decrease the anxiety that occurs when academic standards are vague.
	Students and staff will want and expect class time to be used efficiently.
Support and recognition	Constructive, positive behavior will be given appropriate recognition.
	Positive behavior will be rewarded frequently and publicly when appropriate; rewards will be varied and personal.
	Students and staff will feel appreciated and will receive consistent feedback to reinforce those feelings and behaviors.

Chapter 3

Planning for Safe Schools

Legislative Intent

It is the intent of the Legislature that all California public schools, in kindergarten, and grades 1 to 12, inclusive, operated by school districts, in cooperation with local law enforcement agencies, community leaders, parents, pupils, teachers, administrators, and other persons who may be interested in the prevention of campus crime and violence, develop a comprehensive school safety plan that addresses the safety concerns identified through a systematic planning process.

—Education Code *Section 35294*

SAFE school planning is, of necessity, an ongoing process. The good ideas of one person alone will not achieve a safe school. The long-term success of safe school planning depends on building a community—both within and around the school—that supports critical evaluation of existing conditions and the possibility of change.

Although safe school planning is ultimately a school-site responsibility, there must be support for such efforts from the school district administration, the school board, and the community so that resources are available for program implementation. Therefore, the first step of the planning process focuses on developing a team spirit in the school and surrounding community and a willingness to engage in a continuing process of critical evaluation and change. Without such a team spirit and the willingness continually to assess and revise strategies, safe school planning efforts cannot succeed.

A broad-based safe school committee is the most important element in developing a positive attitude toward critical review and action. Existing school planning committees, such as the School Site Council, may be ideal for addressing safe school planning. The existing team may be broad-based enough to develop and implement the safe school plan after two or three representatives from law enforcement and other community agencies join the team.

Once the committee has created a positive attitude toward change, the members will usually follow a cyclical process similar to the one outlined below:

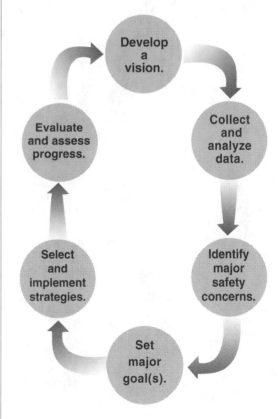

- Develop a vision.
- Collect and analyze data.
- Identify major safety concerns.
- Set major goal(s).
- Select and implement strategies.
- Evaluate and assess progress.

See the accompanying box for an outline of the recommended seven-step safe school planning process. Schools involved in the School Improvement Program (SIP) or other comprehensive re- structuring efforts will note that these steps are similar to those used in most school planning processes. Each step is discussed in detail on the following pages.

Seven-Step Safe School Planning Process

1. **Identify your safe school planning committee members.**
   - Solicit broad representation.
   - Integrate the committee with other school planning and restructuring groups.
   - Promote collaborative planning efforts that include students, parents, and staff.

2. **Create a vision for your school.**
   - Brainstorm and agree on a clear vision of what is to be accomplished.
   - Determine whether the school's current mission statement incorporates the safe school vision.
   - Compare current conditions with the safe school vision.
   - Obtain school and community consensus on the vision.

3. **Gather and analyze information about your school and its community.**
   - Involve parents, students, members of the community, and staff in assessing existing conditions and the climate for action.
   - Review existing data sources from the school, district, and community.
   - Gather objective and subjective quantitative and qualitative data.
   - Inventory resources, including people with expertise.
   - Identify areas of pride and strength.

4. **Identify your school's and community's areas of desired change.**
   - Identify areas needing improvement or change.
   - Explore possible causes of safety concerns.
   - Identify the needs of the school, according to the disparity between what exists and what is desirable.
   - Make a list of high priorities for action.

5. **Set your major goal.**
   - Rank your significant safety concerns.
   - Select the goal or goals to be attained during the academic year.

6. **Select and implement strategies for each safe school component.**
   - Select strategies, actions, and resources to achieve the planning goals for each of the four components.
   - Assign responsibilities, timelines, and completion dates.
   - Develop evaluation criteria and timelines.

7. **Evaluate and assess your progress.**
   - Monitor the implementation of the plan.
   - Determine whether goals are being achieved.
   - Reassess the safe school vision, committee membership, and priorities.

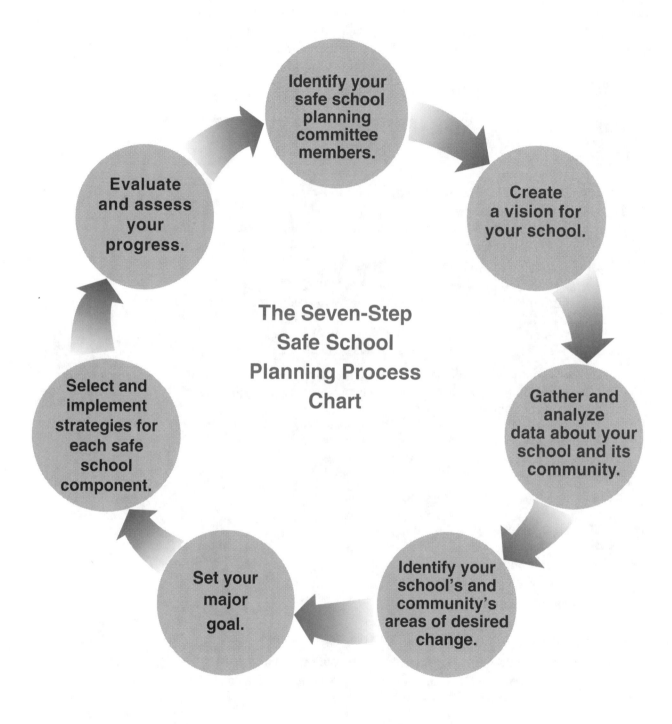

The Seven-Step
Safe School
Planning Process
Chart

Identify your safe school planning committee members.

Create a vision for your school.

Gather and analyze data about your school and its community.

Identify your school's and community's areas of desired change.

Set your major goal.

Select and implement strategies for each safe school component.

Evaluate and assess your progress.

Step 1 Identify Your Safe School Planning Committee Members

A broad-based committee is the cornerstone of a safe school plan. Because of the urgency of safe school problems, principals may be tempted to overlook the need for participatory planning at the site level. The detrimental impact of gangs, drugs, violence, and youthful alienation calls out for immediate action; but most solutions require the committed and shared long-term efforts of school-site personnel, students, parents, media representatives, and community members. Therefore, the school's first step should be to recruit the most effective persons (including administrators, teachers, counselors, security personnel, classified staff, and students) who care about safe school issues and encourage teamwork throughout the planning process. Representatives from law enforcement and juvenile justice agencies, fire departments, health-care programs, parents, the media, and the community are other members crucial to the success of the broad-based safe school committee.

If the school participates in the School Improvement Program or some other school-site planning committee, such as the Healthy Kids and Healthy Start planning committees, restructuring committees, or DATE advisory committees, the safe school committee may be a subcommittee of the larger team; and the safe school plan can become a component of the comprehensive school plan. However, the presence on the safe school subcommittee of community representatives who are knowledgeable about family services, law enforcement, and juvenile justice is crucial. Including representatives of the media is also extremely helpful.

The safe school committee (or subcommittee) must develop its own cultural characteristics and sense of community by sharing perceptions and exchanging ideas. Group leaders must strive to acknowledge and harmonize the diverse concerns and expectations that individuals bring to the planning process. Typically, the people added to an existing school-site planning committee for school safety issues represent agencies outside education. Therefore, the facilitator or chairperson has the added responsibility of developing a committee environment that fosters the active involvement of the newcomers. The better the committee deals with these elements of team building, the stronger its school safety plan will be.

 State Board of Education Policy

It is the policy of the State Board of Education that all students enrolled in public schools in California have the right to attend campuses which are safe and secure. . . . The Board believes that a beginning step toward safer schools is the development of a comprehensive plan for school safety by every public school and district in the state. . . . The Board intends that safe school plans be developed cooperatively by parents, students, teachers, administrators, counselors, and community agencies, including local law enforcement, and approved by the local school district governing board.

—California State Board of Education Policy on School Safety, Discipline, and Attendance

Once the committee is formed, it is important to assess the climate for action. The committee will need to know about student, staff, district, and community attitudes toward school safety, the current safety practices at the school site, and the school's willingness to work toward improvement. By asking people whether their attitudes toward current efforts in school safety are positive, neutral, or negative and how they feel about changing the school safety efforts, the committee can get a measurement of attitudes. A show of hands in group settings or the results of a short questionnaire can provide responses quickly. If the attitudes toward safety and change are positive, the safety planning process will be an easy one. If there are negative attitudes toward change, it is helpful to know what the concerns are and to address them quickly.

While creating and maintaining a positive attitude toward review and action, the safe school committee must begin building the support of important stakeholders, such as the superintendent and other school district administrators, members of local governing boards, and the law enforcement and juvenile justice community. Students and both certificated and classified staff will accept, or "buy in" to, the plans when they participate in the

Not Part of the Team

Sure, I see a lot; but I feel like it's not OK for me to tell them what I see. I'm just an aide; they don't think I know anything. I just feel, you know, less than.

— *Classified Staff Member,*
Voices from the Inside

planning process. The stage is set for action when these groups are aware of and support the safe school planning process.

Step 2   Create a Vision for Your School

Vision building demands positive thinking that emphasizes potential and hope. Vision building allows the safe school committee members to express their desires about how their ideal school community would look, feel, and operate. Creating a vision requires some risk taking and the ability to see the school in a different light. The process of brainstorming and agreeing on the desired outcomes binds together each school and community member of the committee into a team committed to change.

By nature a vision represents the ideal and is not readily achievable in the near future. Before the committee can begin implementing the vision, the committee must relate the vision to the school's existing mission statement. If the mission statement does not reflect the vision, constituent groups, such as the district office, the school board, parents, students, and community agencies, should revise the mission statement to bring it into agreement with the committee's safe school vision. (See Appendix G, Work Sheet 3, for help in relating the school's mission to the group vision.)

Step 3   Gather and Analyze Information About Your School and Its Community

To successfully plan improvements, the safe school committee must first understand the existing conditions at the school. The team must analyze the conditions regularly, using a collection of quantitative data, such as school crime reporting statistics, attendance records, truancy data, accident reports from the school nurse, work orders for vandalism repair, Western Association of Schools and Colleges (WASC) reviews, Program Quality Reviews (PQRs), and community juvenile crime statistics.

Another valuable source of data about the existing conditions in the school is qualitative data, such as attitude surveys of teachers, parents, students, and community members. The data might include a list of areas of pride and strength in the school. Representatives of the media can become powerful allies at this stage of assessing the *perceived* safety concerns of the school because the media often are directly or indirectly responsible for many of the community's attitudes about school safety.

Because such a wealth of information is available, the committee will need to make decisions about which data to collect and study. It is neither necessary nor desirable to collect all types of data, but it is essential to use multiple sources of data to increase the validity of the findings. The analysis should be sufficiently complete so that the committee can make reasonable conclusions and choose future directions.

An important part of this stage of the planning process is to send a message that there is a commitment to make the school safe. The committee can begin creating a positive attitude by letting teachers, students, and others know that their opinions and actions are important. To accomplish this, the committee can conduct personal interviews or surveys and regularly observe campus activities. Through the pro-

School Safety Planning—There Is Hope!

School safety is a priority. I have visited campuses all over the state and have found many individual innovative and effective school safety efforts. Parents, teachers, administrators, and particularly students were all part of programs that have a proven track record of success. So take notice: there is hope out there!

—*Daniel E. Lungren,*
California Attorney General

cess of collecting and analyzing data, the committee increases its knowledge about the problems at the school and begins the process of identifying changes that need to be made.

The following sections describe the kinds of data that are commonly available to safe school committees and suggest ways to use the existing records and new data from questionnaires and observations to develop objectives. (See Appendix G for sample questionnaires and tally sheets and for Work Sheet 4, which can be used to summarize the data collected.)

Existing Records

Relevant existing records include documents and reports required by school policy or law. Schools and law enforcement, juvenile justice, and other social agencies produce the reports regularly. These sources of data are available to safe school committees through interagency cooperation. The following are examples of existing records that relate to school safety:

- School or school district crime incident reports (PC § 628 et seq.)

- Local crime reports and law enforcement records (juvenile crime statistics) (W&IC § 827[b])
- Court and probation information on students committing serious crimes (See Appendix E.)
- Suspension (EC § 48911[e]) and expulsion (EC § 48915) records
- Attendance rates disclosure (EC §§ 48342, 48342.5) and truancy data
- Student progress reports
- School report cards, WASC or PQR reports indicating school needs
- Insurance claims, losses, and risk management data
- School nurse accident reports
- Vandalism work orders

School crime reports. The committee can use school and school district crime statistics to develop an understanding of the most pressing safety issues confronting a school. It is a mistake, however, to rely solely on school crime statistics when developing a safe school plan because of possible errors in reporting procedures or people's reluctance to report data accurately. The American Association of School Administrators notes that schools may not report all school crime incidents because of the concern that such statistics create bad publicity, provide the basis for legal entanglement, or decrease confidence in the school administration.

An important point is that school committees should *not* use the school crime statistics to make cross-district comparisons when reviewing data on school crime. The only reliable and valid comparison that the committee can make is to compare crime rates at the same school or crime rates of schools within the same school district. These comparisons can provide sufficient information for safe

school planning, particularly when the committee asks questions, such as the following:

1. What kinds of crime are reported and in what frequency?
2. Where and when do crimes occur on campus? (Use a plot map to track crimes.)
3. What kinds of persons commit school crimes?
4. What are the characteristics of the students who are chronic offenders?
5. What kinds of persons are most likely to be victims of school crime?
6. Is campus crime a reflection of gang activity?

Local crime reports. Establishing a working partnership with law enforcement agencies and having representatives from those agencies on the safe school committee are invaluable means of gaining access to records that indicate the nature and scope of juvenile crime in the community. School police and law enforcement officials must document incidents of crime. Those records include reports of crimes, arrests, detentions, and investigations. Police reports on juveniles are available to anyone who needs the information for an official disposition of a case (W&IC § 828; for further information see the accompanying box, "Sharing Confidential Information"). Reports on juvenile crimes that occur on the campus may be available to other school authorities under certain circumstances in school districts that have a police or security department. Law enforcement agencies are also required to maintain and report monthly community crime statistics to the state and federal governments. The safe school committee members can ask that those

Sharing Confidential Information

At first glance many agencies' rules seem to make information sharing impossible. However, a close examination of those rules reveals several ways of legally sharing information that will help safety teams make more informed decisions about youths. At the same time students have legitimate privacy concerns about confidential information, and teams must handle the information in a professional manner. Training in the access and proper dissemination of confidential information is necessary as the interagency team implements its information-sharing process.

The courts control access to juvenile court records, probation records, social services records, and school records (see W&IC §§ 826-830 and § 504). Juvenile law enforcement records may be shared with other law enforcement agencies or with any person or agency that has a legitimate need for the information for official disposition of a case (W&IC § 828). Further, if the juvenile court has found that a child has committed a drug offense or a serious violent offense, the court must notify the school staff (W&IC § 827[b] through [e]). Assembly Bill 3786 (Ch. 94-215) allows law enforcement agencies and schools to exchange information. The availability of school records is governed by the federal Family Educational Rights to Privacy Act (20 USC 1232[g]; 34 CFR 99), also called FERPA or the Buckley Amendment, and state statutes that are patterned on FERPA (EC §§ 49061–49077). *Education Code* Section 48267 requires schools to inform the court and probation officer, within 10 days, of any ward of the court who is truant, tardy, or habitually insubordinate. In addition, School Attendance Review Board members have access to school records, as defined in current law (EC § 49076[a] [1]). Recently enacted exchange of information legislation (EC § 49076.5) requires school districts to provide information about a child's identity and location relating to the transfer of the pupil's records when probable cause exists that the pupil has been kidnapped and that the abductor may have enrolled the pupil in school.

Interagency groups that wish to do joint case management and supervision of children involved in the juvenile court process may develop interagency policies and procedures. An excellent example of that kind of activity is the serious habitual offender programs operating in California (W&IC §§ 500–506). These programs have agencies working cooperatively to control juveniles' behavior through improved supervision and services for these active offenders. (AB X 67 authorizes multidisciplinary teams to share otherwise confidential information.)

The simplest and most frequently used method of obtaining records is to have the minor and his or her parents sign a written consent to release records to the requesting agencies. Most schools, probation departments, social services agencies, parole boards, and other agencies have used these consent or waiver forms successfully for years. It is quite rare for anyone to refuse to sign such a consent because parents usually want to cooperate in the service plan for the child involved. Another simple way to share records legally is to obtain a general order from the juvenile court that authorizes interagency record sharing. Juvenile court judges have discretion to issue such orders, commonly known as *TNG* orders (*TNG v. Superior Court* [1971], 4 Cal. 3d 767), releasing juvenile court, school, and other agency records to appropriate agencies for governmental purposes. Each county juvenile court should have a *TNG* order on file, and school staff should obtain a copy. The order can be modified, if necessary, to include all interagency partners working on school safety issues. The court is interested in promoting public safety, in assisting the juvenile justice system to function efficiently, and in basing its own decisions on the best information available. All of these goals can be facilitated with increased access to information by child-serving agencies.

Thorough familiarity with statutes on juvenile and school records, a good working relationship with the juvenile court judge, and an interagency commitment to organized information sharing will allow the school safety program to build a common information base to make better decisions about problem youths and to enhance campus safety for everyone.

crime summaries be made available to the committee. With law enforcement members on the committee, it should be much easier to access those records.

Law enforcement agencies also maintain logs of all calls for assistance from citizens. Such data include the time and location of law enforcement responses to the calls for service. This information may be available in summary form to the safe school committee. Some law enforcement agencies maintain crime analysis units that can provide the committee with more detailed information about the scope and frequency of crime on school campuses and in neighboring communities.

The safe school committee should use its ongoing analysis of local crime reports to answer questions such as these:

1. What types of crime occur on campus or in the community during school hours?

2. Are certain crimes more prevalent on or close to the school campus?

3. Does reduction in truancy result in reduction of daytime crime?

4. Do increased police patrols at night reduce thefts and vandalism on campus?

5. Does adding a school liaison officer reduce calls to police for service?

Court reports and probation information. In California juvenile authorities and schools have a legal responsibility for the mutual reporting of information about students on probation. *Juvenile courts must report to schools within seven days the names of students who have been charged with serious crimes of violence or drug-related offenses* (W&IC § 827[b][2]). *Education Code* Section 48267 requires

courts to notify schools about students who are on probation and requires principals to report a student's truancy violation within 10 days to the student's probation or parole officer. *Education Code* Section 49079 requires school districts to notify teachers about students who have engaged in the activities described in the subdivisions of Section 48900, except for subdivision (h). (See Appendix E for more information on mandatory reporting responsibilities.) The penalty for failure to report such information is one year in jail, a fine of $1,000, or both.

Schools also have reporting responsibilities to courts and other law enforcement agencies. According to *Education Code* Section 48902(a), prior to suspension or expulsion of a student, the school shall report to law enforcement authorities any acts of the student which violate *Penal Code* Section 245 (assault with a deadly weapon). *Education Code* Section 48902(b) requires schools to notify law enforcement authorities, within one school day after the suspension or expulsion of a student, of any act, such as being under the influence of alcohol or drugs, which may violate *Education Code* Section 48900(c) or (d).

In addition, courts may allow schools, probation departments, social service agencies, and the courts to share juvenile justice information (W&IC § 827 and the Family Educational Rights to Privacy Act, 20 USC 1232[g]; see sample Interagency Information Exchange forms in Appendix H). The information can be used to select the most appropriate programs, teachers, and counselors for particular students and thus reduce the potential for further problems.

When collaborating with the courts and probation department, the safe school committee should consider the following questions:

1. How are students' needs best met?

2. Are the interagency partnerships working?

3. Do students on probation need specialized instruction? Counseling?

4. Do parents of students on probation need help? What kind of help?

5. Is school attendance made a priority in probation terms and is attendance enforced?

6. How are probation terms and conditions being enforced?

Suspension and expulsion records. Administrators must keep accurate records of student violations of school rules and procedures (EC §§ 48900 et seq.). These records include dated and signed incident referrals and logs (5 CCR § 431[d]) from teachers and school security personnel; records of disciplinary or counseling responses; and suspension, transfer, and expulsion letters.

The safe school committee can obtain valuable information by examining those records, which are usually summarized annually for the school board. The team can identify specific trends by obtaining answers to these questions:

1. Who makes the disciplinary referrals?

2. Are particular offenses more prevalent at certain grade levels?

3. Are there seasonal variations in the data?

4. What are the common characteristics of students referred for disciplinary action?

5. What academic progress are these students making? Are "D" and "F" lists used? How are they used?

6. Are these students achieving in any subject area? Why?

7. Is there a racial or ethnic overtone to the numbers of suspensions and expulsions?

8. Are law enforcement agencies informed about disciplinary incidents that are also crimes?

9. Do the above reports reflect information included in the school crime report?

10. Are the *Education Code* sections on children with Individualized Educational Programs (IEPs) being observed?

11. Are children with IEPs provided with home instruction when suspended or expelled? (See *Honig v. Doe*, 484 U.S. 305 [1988].)

It may be helpful to ask the principal to provide summaries and analyses of the data as well as recommendations based on the data.

Attendance and truancy data. By law all students between six and eighteen years of age must attend school (EC § 48200), yet absenteeism is a major concern in many schools. Because school funding is largely determined by daily attendance, school districts keep detailed, often computerized records. These attendance records are readily available to the safe school committee and provide a comprehensive picture of attendance patterns. The records enable districts to track attendance and aggressively intervene when students become habitual truants (EC §§ 48260 et seq.).

School districts frequently prepare reports summarizing activities that are designed to deal with habitually truant students. When cases involve the School

Attendance Review Board (SARB), the deputy district attorneys, and probation officers, the safe school committee would probably find those records useful. Committees should use attendance and truancy data to answer questions such as the following:

1. What are the most common reasons for absences?
2. Is there a daily or weekly pattern of class cuts? Have reasons been suggested and preventive recommendations made? Are these available?
3. Are there seasonal variations in attendance patterns?
4. Is the SARB or the truancy mediation program an effective resource? What is its success rate at the school?
5. Is there a correlation between absenteeism and crime patterns in the community?

Attendance Reporting

The governing board of each school district shall annually disclose to the public the actual pupil attendance rates for each school in the district and certify to the Superintendent of Public Instruction that the requirement has been met (EC §§ 48342, 48342.5). The county board of education may require all private and public schools in the county to submit attendance severance reports and may review those cases needing further examination (EC § 48202).

6. Do truancy cases go to court? How many went to court last year?
7. Are probation officers notified when students on probation are absent or truant?
8. Does the probation department enforce all the terms of a juvenile's probation?
9. Are there examples of collaborative work between the school and probation department?

Student progress reports. Schools maintain a wide variety of information about students' academic progress, including letter grades, test scores, and citizenship ratings. Schools use the records to refine the instructional program and to evaluate its impact on student development. While respecting students' rights to confidentiality, the safety committee can use the information to examine trends in student performance and adjustment and provide answers to the following questions:

1. What are the common characteristics of students who experience success in school compared with students who are on the "D" and "F" lists?
2. What is the relationship between students' academic progress and school crime, students' attendance, and other data reflecting unsafe school conditions?
3. What are the grade point averages of students with records of poor discipline and criminal behavior?
4. What is the relationship between poor academic progress and involvement in school crime?

School report cards. It may be informative for the safe school committee to re-

All children between six and eighteen years of age must attend school full time unless exempted under certain provisions of the *Education Code* (EC § 48200). Children not subject to compulsory full-time education must attend school on at least a part-time basis until they are eighteen years old, have graduated, are enrolled in another educational program, or are otherwise exempted (EC §§ 48200 et seq.).

When students are absent without valid excuse for more than three days or tardy more than 30 minutes daily for more than three days in one school year, those students are truant and must be reported to the attendance supervisor or to the superintendent of the district (EC § 48260). In addition, the school district must notify the students' parents or guardians of the truancy, their obligation to compel the students' attendance at school, and the consequence of the failure to meet that obligation (EC § 48260.5). When a student is reported truant three or more times per school year, that student is classified as a habitual truant. Staff must have made a conscientious effort to contact the parents and to hold at least one conference with them and with the pupil before deeming the pupil an habitual truant (EC §§ 48261, 48262). Habitual truants and their parents may be dealt with by the School Attendance Review Board (SARB) or by a truancy mediation program run by the county probation department or district attorney (EC §§ 48260.6, 48263–48295, 48320–48325). If those interventions do not succeed in resolving the problem, the pupil may be referred to juvenile court for prosecution (WIC §§ 601(b), 601.1-601.4), and the parent may be cited to municipal court and ordered to pay a fine (EC §§ 48290–48293).

The California Supreme Court issued two opinions supporting truancy procedures. One case affirms the ability of law enforcement authorities to work with schools on truancy abatement programs by detaining suspected truants and returning them to school (*In re James D.* [1987], 43 Cal. 3d 903, 239 Cal. Rptr. 663). The other case allows a student to be incarcerated briefly if he or she has been declared a ward of the juvenile court because of truancy, has been ordered to attend school, then defies the court's order (*In re Michael G.* [1988], 44 Cal. 3d 283, 243 Cal. Rptr. 224). When police and school officials make sure that students are in school, community crime problems decrease, and the chances of getting to the root of a student's attendance problems increase. Once the student is back in an educational setting, the school may use outreach methods, special tutoring, counseling, and other interventions to prevent further truancy and to help keep the student from dropping out of school entirely.

Strong and active SARBs report 70 to 90 percent success rates in getting students and parents to cooperate in improving the students' attendance. Although many steps are required in the SARB or truancy mediation process, systematic follow-through will usually bring results.

When the pupil and parent do not comply with the process, interagency cooperation is necessary to carry out the prosecution phase. It is important for the agencies to work out the formal procedures necessary for the probation officer to process the student and for the district attorney to prosecute the parent. Both the probation officer and the district attorney make a last attempt to gain the cooperation of the pupil and the parent to clear up the attendance problem. If the attempt fails, the case goes to court.

In jurisdictions that have not taken many such cases to court, several face-to-face meetings may be necessary to establish working relationships between agencies and to get the necessary commitment from each to create a formalized court process. After all agencies have agreed on the best procedure, policies should be drafted for everyone to follow; and the staff involved in preparing cases for court should be trained to follow the policies and procedures correctly. By doing so, the parents or student will be held accountable by the judge when the case gets to court.

view the annual school report card or other reports on the general condition of the school and its educational programs. For example, the PQR, WASC, Coordinated Compliance Review, or other reports that evaluate the school's performance may provide significant information about areas of need within the school's programs. If the school safety committee is not a part of the School Improvement Program, the committee may need to interview the SIP leadership team to determine the areas that it has identified as needing improvement.

Insurance claims, losses, and risk management data. School district superintendents should have access to accident reports, insurance claims, and reports of liability issues and losses. Such information may be summarized in reports that the safety team can use to understand issues relevant to the safety of a particular school. For example, responses to the following questions are important:

1. What are the most frequent and the most costly loss and liability issues of the school?
2. What is the annual liability loss to the district?

Begin Truancy Prevention in Elementary Schools

Truancy prevention programs should be developed in every elementary school so that at the first sign of truancy, police, social service agencies, and the school can join together to identify the cause and do something about it before it is too late.

—*U.S. Attorney General Janet Reno,*
quoted in Juvenile Justice, *Fall/Winter, 1993*

3. Are staff informed about the proper procedures for filing accident reports?
4. Are certain schools the sites of more frequent or costly claims or losses?
5. Are there recurring patterns in the claims or losses made against the district or school?

Accident reports. It is important to review accident reports to determine whether any patterns of injuries exist that might indicate school safety concerns. In schools that have a health center or nurse, the records will be easier to obtain. In other schools the principal or secretary is the most likely person to keep an accident log.

Vandalism work orders. The school vandalism work orders provide an excellent source of information that the safety committee can examine for an accurate picture of the extent and cost of vandalism. These work orders are generally completed by staff on site and forwarded to the maintenance and operation personnel. The work orders contain details about the type and location of vandalism incidents. When completed, the reports show actual repair costs. By reviewing these documents, the committee may be able to identify important patterns and trends. For example, are there particular types of vandalism (e.g., graffiti) that consistently recur? Are there specific times of the day or week that the vandalism occurs? Are certain locations more vulnerable than others? It is important for the committee to determine whether the trends that are identified indicate that additional security measures, such as lighting, fences, school police, or security personnel, might be appropriate. Reviewing work orders also ensures that the committee has an accurate picture of the complete costs resulting from acts of vandalism. Knowing the significant cost of materials and labor involved in the repair and cleanup of vandalism is an important element in assessing the full impact that vandalism has on a school campus.

New Data

As discussed earlier, qualitative data (e.g., observations of campus conditions and attitude surveys of teachers, parents, students, and community members) are important sources of information in safe school planning. Questionnaires and surveys allow people to express their opinions confidentially. After reviewing large samples of questionnaires, the safe school committee can identify group trends with reasonable accuracy. However, good questionnaires are difficult to construct, and their accuracy is greatly dependent on the cooperation of the respondents.

A series of questionnaires and tally sheets is provided in Appendix G to assist the safe school committee in evaluating adult and student perceptions of the safety levels related to each of the four safe school components described in Chapter 2. The committee may modify the forms to address the particular needs and issues of individual schools. The process will increase the committee members' awareness of the many complex issues involved in a safe school and familiarize the members with the various instruments and procedures available for assessing the school climate.

In addition to the questionnaires, observations of the behavior of students and staff can reveal much about how safe they feel their school is. Informal observations may involve a casual look at one or more programs or conditions, followed by a brief report. This method provides information without obvious intrusion in day-to-day campus activities. (See Appendix G, Tally Sheet 3, for a model that can be used for such observations.)

Finally, the committee should identify areas of pride and strength (see Appendix G, Work Sheet 4). This step will help the committee build on positive programs that are working and provide students and staff with a sense that they have been doing some things *right.* It is important to show people that their efforts leading up to the work of the committee were not in vain.

Step 4 | Identify Your School's and Community's Areas of Desired Change

After collecting the extensive subjective and objective data described in step 3, the committee is prepared to identify areas of desired change. This step should be revisited regularly as part of the ongoing assessment strategy. Identifying the major areas of desired change helps the committee prepare for its next step—that of identifying priorities for action. (Work Sheet 5 in Appendix G is designed to help the committee complete the tasks in step 4.)

The committee will need to consider comments from the community in identifying and prioritizing major concerns. A survey of the local chamber of commerce, board of realtors, and other active community groups, agencies, and leaders will provide that information.

Although the particular processes that each safe school committee uses to make its decisions will vary, the committee must accomplish the following tasks during this stage of safe school planning:

1. Identify areas needing improvement or change.
2. Explore the possible causes of safety concerns.
3. Identify the needs of the school according to the disparity between what exists and that which is desirable.
4. Make a list of high priorities for action (consensus).

Conflict Resolution

Four years ago, most of the 1,500 sixth, seventh, and eighth graders [at Roosevelt Middle School in Oceanside, California] lived in fear as gangs "mad dogged" each other–deliberately provoking fights. Today, the school is a placid oasis thanks to a plan called "Resolving Conflict Creatively." First, the curriculum was infused with instruction on listening attentively, dealing with anger, and overcoming racial stereotypes. Then a system of peer mediation was started. When a problem develops, it usually is settled within a day by student mediators who are trained to sit classmates down and resolve arguments with words rather than fists. Typically, one student threatens another, but they agree to avoid a confrontation until their anger passes. . . . "We want to weave conflict resolution into the fabric of everyone's educational experience, " says Larry Dieringer of Educators for Social Responsibility, which helps run Resolving Conflict Creatively in 225 schools nationwide. Despite the program's popularity, there isn't much proof yet that it significantly reduces school crime. The federal Centers for Disease Control and Prevention is spending $2.4 million to study its effects.

— U.S. News & World Report
November 8, 1993

Step 5   Set Your Major Goal

Now the committee is ready to set one or more broad goals that address the highest priorities for action and, when implemented, will lead to achieving the vision. The committee should be realistic and set only one or two goals that are achievable in a year's time. (See Appendix G, Work Sheet 6.) Otherwise, if committee members are overly ambitious in setting more goals than they may possibly achieve in one year, the team and the school community will face disappointment and perhaps disillusionment with the process.

Step 6   Select and Implement Strategies for Each Safe School Component

After reviewing the data and setting the goal(s), the committee is ready to develop an action plan—one that will detail what will need to be done to make the school better and safer. To ensure a comprehensive plan, the committee should:

1. Select objectives, activities, and resources that address each of the four components described in Chapter 2. (If more than one goal is chosen, this procedure will need to be followed for each of the goals.) See Appendix G for Work Sheets 7A through 7D, which are designed to help the team formulate its action plan for each component; a sample action plan for component 1 is presented in Work Sheet 7E.
2. Identify and work with other programs and plans that share common goals. (See Appendix B for charts

showing the major curricular and school reform strands.)

3. Assign responsibilities, timelines, and completion dates.
4. Develop evaluation criteria and timelines.

In the pressure to improve school safety, schools are tempted to respond only to campus crises as they arise rather than to look for the root of the problems and prevent the crises in the first place. However, it is important for the committee to choose objectives and activities that work on three levels: prevention, intervention, and restructuring.

Prevention efforts are those actions and programs designed to prevent problems before they occur. Sample prevention actions might include developing a curriculum emphasizing personal and social skills in the early grades; preparing antidrug and antigang curricula for the early grades; closing campuses; installing alarms; inspecting campuses and having a walk-through with fire and police personnel to identify potential hazards; training staff to recognize problems; and adopting peer-counseling and peer-advising programs.

Intervention efforts are actions and programs designed to reduce or eliminate existing problems. Sample intervention actions might include alternative education programs; reentry for dropouts; parenting classes; conflict resolution; gang violence- and drug-suppression programs; intensive supervision of juvenile offenders, involving school staff working closely with probation officers; programs for latchkey children; a strong district SARB; training for staff in managing assaultive behavior and conducting proper searches for drugs and weapons; and

Respect

I had to redefine some things for me because I thought respect was what I wanted. In the gang they teach you that if people disrespect you, you act in a violent way to earn power and control. I learned another way was to respect people, and respect is being treated like you want to be treated and treating other people the same way, and that isn't with a gun. I've been on both sides of the barrel, and I didn't like the feeling.

—*Francesco Gallardo, age twenty,* Denver, Kids in the Crossfire, *ABC News*

group problem-solving classes for selected staff members. School counselors, when available, are excellent at implementing such programs. When no school counselor is available, or when the counselor needs additional resources, the team can call on community resources, such as alternative placement centers or mental health or other youth-serving social agencies, to design and implement intervention efforts.

Restructuring efforts are long-term, comprehensive strategies designed to reorganize an entire school. Schools can use many restructuring strategies individually as prevention efforts. Sample restructuring actions might include the following:

- Homerooms offering specialized instruction (e.g., programs on nonviolence, self-esteem, conflict resolution, drug and alcohol education)
- Regular off-site staff development sessions for teachers and support personnel
- Schoolwide policies on such matters as homework, dress, and conduct that

include requiring parents and students to sign contracts agreeing to adhere to the policies

- Regularly scheduled student assemblies and workshops that address such issues as gangs, multicultural relations, drugs, and self-esteem
- Regular programs on campus in which law enforcement and juvenile justice personnel are involved with students and staff (e.g., training, counseling, resource referral, speaking, interagency case management teams)
- School safety training courses for teachers and administrators
- A media campaign to promote a good image of the school in the community
- A school safety resource center located at the district office

As the safe school committee identifies its own priority issues, it must choose actions and strategies that work on three levels: preventing problems, intervening in existing problems, and restructuring the system when a comprehensive approach is necessary. Schools can design most programs to overlap all three levels in a coordinated approach that will not only address current needs but also direct future planning.

Step 7   Evaluate and Assess Your Progress

Assessment and evaluation are necessary and *ongoing* components of any program plan. An evaluation strategy will enable the committee to monitor progress and give direction for adjusting strategies as the project enters new phases. The ultimate aim of an evaluation strategy is to determine the effectiveness of the plan

in achieving the results that are stated in the original goal.

The ongoing assessment process should involve monitoring the implementation of the plan; that is, assessing the progress in meeting timelines and objectives. Another important aspect of the assessment is determining whether the committee asked the right questions when it specified areas of desired change. If progress is clearly "out of sync" with the goals and objectives, the committee may have made assumptions that steered the plan away from important issues.

The evaluation process should include assessing improvements made in relation to each of the components of a safe school plan. Assessing objectives by component will ultimately lead to an analysis of the progress in meeting the major goal(s) and achieving the vision (see Appendix G, Work Sheets 9 and 10). The safe school committee is accountable for the effects and outcomes of the plan. Knowing that the planned strategies and actions are working will validate the committee's decision making, build confidence among committee members, and direct future planning and action.

As part of the program evaluation, the committee should cross-check to ensure that it has covered all aspects of school life, including curriculum, staff development, social and recreational events, parental involvement programs, family services, discipline and guidance, and crisis response plans. The committee should work with other school planning groups to integrate safe school planning whenever possible.

The committee membership should be reviewed regularly (step 1) to determine whether new representatives from

Building a Comprehensive Strategy

The Modesto city schools have been developing a comprehensive partnership approach to their school safety concerns for the past several years. The main components of their strategy include the following:

1. Every school site has a safety committee, which is composed of an interagency team. The sites must send a revised version of their safety plan to the school district office each year.

2. Through a contract with the city police department, two full-time officers are assigned to the school district. The advantages of this arrangement are numerous. Perhaps most important is the information sharing that occurs naturally as a result of the contract. For instance, officers are briefed at a Monday staff meeting prior to the opening of school. The school district quickly learns about altercations or other community events that have the potential of "spilling over" to the schools. Because of the close relationship with the police department, the school district also has access to all units of the department, such as gang suppression.

3. The school district has a similar contractual arrangement with the Stanislaus County Probation Department. The advantages of information sharing are similar to those of cooperating with the police department.

4. The school district has a full-time gang prevention officer to visit all campuses daily.

5. The Project Y.E.S. curriculum has been used for three years.

6. "Operation Stay in School" has been extremely successful. In a recent case the officer picking up a suspected truant found the student armed with a semiautomatic weapon.

7. According to school district officials, the close relationships with community police and family service agencies allow the district to respond more quickly to potential crises. Instead of being in a "911" response mode, the school district's partners are often the first to alert the district to potential problems.

8. Through a "Healthy Start" grant, the school district was able to place full-service family health centers on two campuses (one elementary school and one middle school). The centers offer full-time doctors, dentists, and mental health professionals through agreements with community partners. At one school the center is placed across from the housing authority and low-income family housing; as a result many other family services are being offered on that campus, including preschool and day care. The community feels proud of its school, which serves as a community center. The community's concern for the school helps ensure its safety.

9. An extensive Police Activities League program serves more than 1,000 children in the district's K–8 schools. In the program volunteer police officers work with the youngsters to build rapport and self-esteem.

For more information, contact Sharon Rohrke, Assistant Superintendent, Modesto City Elementary and High School Districts; telephone 209-576-4041.

the related agencies should be recruited to meet new objectives. Depending on the ongoing monitoring of progress, the committee may need to review new data (step 3) and reprioritize major safety concerns (step 4).

The act of safe school planning itself sends a positive schoolwide message that it is important to acknowledge problems and work together to solve them. Safe school planning leads to greater trust and interdependence among teachers, students, parents, administrators, and community representatives and lasting commitments to creating and maintaining safe, secure, and peaceful schools in which students can reach their maximum academic potential.

The Need to Be Valued

Every young person needs feelings of self-worth, identity, acceptance, recognition, companionship, belonging, purpose, and security. When families, schools, churches, and communities cannot meet those needs, gangs may.

—*From* On Alert! Gang Prevention:
School In-Service Guidelines

Chapter 4

Safe School Strategies and Actions

Success of Peer Mediation Programs

Society has glorified violence as a way to solve problems. Movies, music, and even television cartoons send the message that violence is the quickest and most effective way to solve a conflict. Young people who are using school-based conflict resolution programs are learning to talk out problems, rather than fight or shoot them out. Mediation is a viable solution to confrontation. It is an alternative to violence. It is encouraging to see the success many of these programs are having in promoting these alternatives.

—*Daniel E. Lungren*
California Attorney General

B Y following the planning process discussed in the preceding chapter, the safe school committee can systematically evaluate the safety issues confronting the school and identify the major problems it wants to solve to improve the school's safety environment. Some of the problems may have simple solutions, such as installing a light

in a dark hallway or removing lockers. Many problems may be far more complex and may require more time and resources; a long-term commitment of staff, students, and parents; and the cooperation of community agencies to reach the desired goal—a safe campus. Through the development of a school safety plan that incorporates prevention programs, intervention programs, and restructuring when necessary, even those schools with complex problems can solve them by coordinating their efforts.

The school's ability to build bridges to other community agencies and develop a true team effort with law enforcement and juvenile justice agencies and the community is crucial to the plan's success. This team effort must include timely interagency communication and training of all the members to ensure cooperative, coordinated planning and implementation of strategic actions. While the school safety plan is solving the problem, it is also promoting and enhancing a positive learning environment.

Because there are more than 5.25 million students in California's 7,731 public schools and 1,002 school districts, it is not feasible to create one universal, statewide safe school plan. Therefore, the safe school committee of each school must design or modify existing programs and strategies to meet the specific concerns of that school. The design and content of the action plan need to reflect the nature and intensity of the school's unique problems, which are identified during the planning process. Initially, some schools will focus on basic safety issues, and others will move immediately to improve the teaching-learning environment.

Furthermore, there are only about 226 unified school districts. Consequently, in a majority of school districts, the high schools and their feeder schools need to develop a unified approach so that they can deal with families, social agencies, the juvenile justice system, and disciplinary issues in a consistent manner.

This chapter presents many ideas designed to help safe school committees address needs in each of the four components of a safe school environment: the personal characteristics of students and staff, the school's physical environment, the school's social environment, and the school's culture. Committees should devise strategies addressing each of those components for each goal that is identified.

The following lists of potential actions are not exhaustive but will provide the safe school committee with many suggestions for creating its particular school safety plan. When devising strategies to meet the chosen goal(s), the safe school committee should ensure that safety is an integral part of the general school plan and that the plan addresses the following areas:

- Crisis response
- Curriculum
- Discipline
- Family services
- Guidance and counseling
- Parental involvement
- Social and recreational events
- Staff development

The committee will want to ensure that all school and community program personnel are aware of strategies that affect them; support the safe school efforts; and are involved, whenever appropriate.

Strategies and Actions for Component 1

The following suggestions relate to the *personal characteristics of students and staff*.

Ethnic and Cultural Diversity, Life Experiences, Health Concerns

To achieve safe schools, educators and agency personnel must first believe that safety is possible for *all* students and staff, regardless of the demographic and social conditions affecting the schools. Safe school planning must take into account the ethnic, racial, cultural, and religious backgrounds of the students. Through leadership, curriculum reform, and special instructional activities, schools can respect the diverse backgrounds of all students. Schools can use cross-cultural programs to teach staff and students about the history, heritage, and culture of all groups on campus. Schools can design bilingual programs, ESL classes, and orientation and guidance programs to assist new students in adjusting to their new environment.

Ideas for developing programs that respect the diversity, life experiences, and health concerns of the students and staff are as follows:

1. Track demographic data in the school district and at each school site.
2. Counter biases and stereotypical perceptions by providing information in the school curriculum about the heritage of various students and staff

Cultural Barriers

I am sensitive to cultural barriers that exist among educators. These barriers are created by lack of communication between people coming from different backgrounds and cultures. We don't discuss cultural conflicts openly. We have learned that conflicts are negative and produce racial disharmony when, in fact, the opposite is true.

—*Latina elementary teacher,*
Voices from the Inside

and developing cross-cultural experiences and programs.

3. Recognize cultural and ethnic holidays observed in the community. Hold a "history week" and special events to commemorate important dates.

4. Invite cultural and ethnic community groups to hold events on school campuses in the evenings and on weekends.

5. Recruit a teaching and counseling staff that reflects the ethnic and racial makeup of the school community.

6. Recruit a parent coordinator who can communicate well with the ethnic groups that are represented in the school. Encourage the development of programs that invite parents to be part of the school community. For example, provide training so that parents may participate in the classroom; offer parenting classes to improve parents' child-rearing abilities; provide a regular forum for parents to express concerns; and provide opportunities for involvement in school safety improvement projects.

7. Conduct thorough background checks on potential school district employees.

8. Require the child welfare and attendance supervisor or other administrator to screen and develop a program to monitor all students who are returning to school from a juvenile court placement or who have been expelled from another school district.

9. Develop school liaisons with child-serving and child-protective agencies. Establish procedures for referrals and for exchanging information between the school and the students' caseworkers. Participate, when appropri-

ate, in child abuse multidisciplinary teams; share information for early intervention. Encourage social workers, mental health practitioners, probation officers, and other allied agency personnel to make school attendance a priority in the supervision of students' cases.

10. Coordinate with county health services to use school facilities for health clinics and related services, such as exercise, dieting, cessation of smoking, stress reduction, and similar health improvement programs.

Staff Expertise

Safe school planning addresses the need for a balanced and diversified staff that effectively meets the needs of the student body. Both recruitment and in-service training programs will help in achieving the balance. Accurately assessing the background and needs of the students and providing the necessary in-service training and support systems for staff are the more complex issues. Staff must be aware of the social issues confronting their students (especially if staff members live in different communities), participate in the latest and most effective training to meet those needs, and demonstrate respect for and sensitivity to the students they teach. The following list provides suggestions for developing staff expertise:

1. Coordinate school safety and school law workshops for staff. Use interagency instructors from school, law enforcement, juvenile justice, social services, mental health, protective services, and other agencies to teach workshops on conducting search and seizure activities, handling intruders, managing assaultive behavior, man-

aging anger, responding to a crisis, reporting child abuse, reporting crime, preventing crime, preventing suicide, improving self-esteem, developing cross-cultural relations, preventing and treating drug and alcohol abuse, and so forth. Include administrators, counselors, teachers, clerical staff, substitute teachers, aides, bus drivers, custodial staff, and security staff in the trainings. Videotape workshops so that new employees may review the material as part of their school-site and school district orientation.

2. Encourage colleges and universities to include school safety topics in their curriculum for teacher, administrator, and counselor education programs.

3. Develop a teacher's handbook with basic school safety information.

4. Offer first-aid and CPR (cardiopulmonary resuscitation) classes to students and staff. Teach students and staff techniques to avoid placing themselves at risk of attack or property loss.

5. Encourage students, staff, and parents to form campus safety groups.

6. Create a school safety resource library in the school district or county office.

Strategies and Actions for Component 2

The following suggestions relate to the *school's physical environment.*

School Location

Location refers to the setting of the school within its community or neighborhood. Although the school team cannot

A Safe and Healthy Environment

Above all a safe and healthy school environment ensures that the school is a haven from the violence many young people encounter elsewhere. Such an environment is one that is well maintained and is free of such hazards as asbestos dust or drinking water contaminated by lead. A plan to be implemented in case of fire or natural disasters or other emergencies should be well rehearsed. In addition, lavatories and other sanitary facilities should be kept clean, supplied with soap and towels, and maintained well; play equipment should be inspected for safety at regular intervals; and the school grounds should be monitored and kept free of alcohol, tobacco, and other drugs.

—Health Framework for California Public Schools

readily alter this factor, safe school planning can identify potential problems and develop responses and programs to counteract them. For example, if a campus is physically separated from the community, the school can do much to make itself an integral part of the community through interagency efforts and community activities. Illustrations of actions to enhance the school's location are as follows:

1. Create a committee of school staff, students, parents, citizens, and law enforcement officers to identify safe routes on which students can travel to and from school. Set up block-parent or safe-business networks along those routes and provide screening and training for parents or proprietors who wish to participate.

2. Form a Neighborhood Watch program, using the school as the meeting place, and provide child care. Teach residential security and encourage volunteers to assist with school observation and crime reporting.

3. Consider proposing zoning statutes that would establish a minimum distance from campus for the location of certain types of businesses, such as liquor stores and fast food restaurants, that often act as magnets for peripheral illegal activities.

School Grounds

One of the most visible aspects of a safe school environment is the quality of the security and maintenance of the school grounds. The safety and appearance of the school grounds are likely to make an im-

Interagency Teamwork

Too much time, energy, and scarce fiscal resources are being spent devising procedures for guarding the security of students, staff, and property. At a minimum, state and local governments must assume full responsibility for providing law enforcement services in and near our schools, just as they now furnish fire protection services. Further, schools must be integrated into local emergency networks and tied into interagency health and safety networks—with up-to-date telecommunications systems.

— *Del Weber*
President of the California Teachers Association, in Rediscovering Education: Creating Schools for the 21st Century

mediate impression on students, parents, and visitors from the community. The four primary concerns involved in the safety of school grounds are securing the campus perimeter, maintaining hazard-free grounds, minimizing vandalism, and creating a safe and inviting appearance. Illustrations of actions contributing to the safety of the school grounds are as follows:

1. Install signs required by law regarding school trespassing violations. Require identification tags for all school visitors. Train and encourage staff to approach people on campus who are not wearing identification tags and to refer them to the office.

2. Limit places for loitering; for example, patrol bathrooms and locker areas. Consider eliminating student lockers at schools with a high incidence of drug or weapons offenses.

3. Maximize unobstructed views by eliminating blind spots caused by doorways, fences, support buildings, storage containers, and landscaping. Eliminate possibilities for easy roof access. Install appropriate doors, windows, locks, and fixtures.

4. Plan beautification projects involving students, staff, and citizens. For example, secure donations of seeds, flowers, shrubs, or sculptures from local nurseries, garden clubs, service clubs, and city parks departments.

5. Hold Saturday litter pickups involving students, staff, and citizens.

6. Organize crews of students, staff, parents, and citizens to clean up the sidewalks and streets around the school.

7. Improve communication among school police or security personnel, teachers, students, and the school of-

fice. Provide incentives for the entire staff and student body to take responsibility for keeping the school safe.

8. Request a risk management or safety assessment walk-through and audit by law enforcement personnel, the fire marshal, and insurance consultants. Minimize conditions on campus that could cause accidental injuries.

9. Develop live-in security or custodial arrangements.

10. Create incentives among school groups to reduce vandalism and share the cost savings with them.

11. Cover graffiti and repair damage immediately. Use crews of students, staff, parents, and citizens for removal of graffiti. Ask business or community groups to donate paint.

12. Increase the presence on campus of school liaison law enforcement officers, probation officers, and other child-oriented agency personnel.

13. When doing rehabilitation, relocation, or remodeling, consider environmental design concepts that foster adequate supervision and promote physical safety.

School Buildings and Classrooms

Safe school plans must ensure that buildings and classrooms are well maintained and attractive, free of obvious physical hazards, and designed to prevent undetected criminal activities. The following actions will increase the safety of buildings and classrooms:

1. Learn proven "target hardening" techniques from crime prevention experts to make the school buildings less vulnerable to break-ins or damage. Make it harder for the criminal to do the crime.

Students Concerned About Violence

The threat of fights, stabbings, or shootings leaves many students less than engrossed in science or history. "Kids didn't want to go to class, they couldn't eat or sleep, they burst out crying," says Jettie Tisdale, principal of Longfellow Elementary School in Bridgeport, Connecticut, of the days after two students were gunned down outside the school last January. . . . So many bullets were flying at Longfellow from the P. T. Barnum housing project next door that bulletproof windows were installed on one side of the school. Says Tisdale: "We couldn't think about teaching reading, writing, and arithmetic until we dealt with these problems."

—U.S. News & World Report, November 8, 1993

2. Involve students, staff, law enforcement officials, and school police or security personnel in reviewing designs for new schools.

3. Involve students and parents in projects to decorate buildings and classrooms in an inviting and pleasing manner.

4. Solicit support from community businesses to provide materials to improve the school's appearance.

Internal Security Procedures

Internal security policies and procedures are crucial aspects of safe school planning. Effective procedures provide for an orderly campus where students are in class or other appropriate environments and intruders cannot enter. The following

Where Students Feel Safe

My perfect school is where they have a place after school for kids to wait so they won't get stolen by strangers.

—Elementary student,
Voices from the Inside

ideas may prove helpful in designing internal security procedures:

1. Schedule interagency meetings with law enforcement and other community agencies to plan for potential campus crises, such as earthquakes, homicides, suicide attempts, bomb threats, and weapons on campus. Discuss leadership, logistics, access routes, and related issues.

2. Review the building security system. Do an assessment with experts to determine whether the system needs improvement.

3. Develop strategies that enable students to participate in school crime prevention activities. In some schools the formation of a school watch committee in each classroom may encourage students to report suspicious activities to school officials and parents. In other schools an anonymous reporting system, such as a telephone hot line, will be more effective in overcoming the code of silence among students.

4. Provide campus security personnel with appropriate training, in coordination with law enforcement agencies. For example, training may be given on days when teachers are receiving staff development activities (EC §§ 44680 et seq.).

5. Design an information system that provides daily information on school crimes, intrusions, accidents, or other safety problems on campus. Develop a standardized report form on which personnel can readily record all such school incidents. Analyze the data for use in preventive activities and proactive measures that are included in the school action plan.

6. Train staff in school crime reporting procedures and monitor statistics closely.

7. Promote development of school district policies and procedures to ensure accurate school crime reporting to the state and local law enforcement agencies. Obtain interagency suggestions on the types of crime that should be reported to law enforcement officers. Use school crime statistics for action planning.

8. Institute a closed-campus policy.

9. Regularly patrol locations on campus in which students are known to congregate when they cut class or those in which illegal activities take place. Set up a supervision map of the school to monitor these problem areas.

10. Regularly patrol nearby areas in which truant students might congregate. If students are found, transport them back to school or to the truancy center. Increase the frequency of after-hour patrols of the vicinity of the school.

11. Consider removing lockers to control contraband and reduce the number of weapons being brought to school.

12. Encourage after-school, evening, and weekend use of school facilities by community organizations, the adult school, and athletic groups. The more the school is occupied, the more it is watched.

13. Mark all school property with permanent identification marks or numbers. Keep an itemized inventory of all school equipment, including serial numbers.

14. Strictly control access to keys.

15. Make regular reports on school crime and safety data at public school board meetings.

16. Support student and parental involvement at school board meetings and school advisory meetings.

17. Ask school-site or school district risk managers to consider applying through their self-insurance pool for safety credits to help finance employee safety measures, purchase disaster supplies, or provide staff training on safety issues.

Strategies and Actions for Component 3

The following suggestions relate to the *school's social environment.*

Leadership

Safe schools are ones in which there is a sense of commitment from students, parents, staff, and the community. However, it is important for the principal and his or her administrative team to provide strong leadership in setting a vision and action plan and in sharing the decision-making with staff, parents, students, school police or security personnel, and community leaders. The active involvement of the school's leaders in school activities provides the direction necessary to set a positive tone in the school. The following are suggestions to help build a strong leadership team:

1. Learn and use the names of students in positive and supportive settings.

2. Develop a team approach through shared decision making to address all major issues.

3. Identify student leaders (formal and informal); include them regularly in activities that build positive student involvement.

4. Involve the district superintendent and school board in school safety efforts. Invite them to participate in site visits and a safety walk-through of the school.

5. Regularly walk the campus and visit classrooms. Be highly visible in the cafeteria and at transportation loading points.

6. Respond personally to concerns of students, parents, and staff. Make time for any student, parent, or staff member who wants to meet with you.

7. Attend at least one meeting of each campus organization every year.

8. Develop a team approach to identifying conditions, such as suspicious group movements or activities, that signify problems. Be there and step in. Develop an information network to keep up on what happens in the school neighborhood during the weekend.

9. Act on rumors. Talk to students whenever you hear rumors that they are involved in problems. Direct them to counseling and diversionary

programs that will help them to avoid improper behavior. Contact parents when necessary. Document all meetings and phone calls.

10. Enlist the help of the staff and student body in continuously promoting the belief and commitment that the school is a safe, orderly place. Make sure that students and the community know that the school is neutral territory.

11. Assign those teachers, counselors, and bus drivers who are skilled in conflict management and have excellent interpersonal skills to the most difficult students, classes, or bus routes.

12. Encourage staff members to be visible in the community; for example, by attending city council meetings and joining community service clubs.

School-Site Management

The administrative structure of a safe school is open and flexible rather than closed and rigid. In such a school, students, parents, staff, and the community are involved in setting school goals and in providing comments and suggestions on school policies and procedures. This kind of open organization helps students, parents, and staff feel that they have some control over their destiny because they have an opportunity to make choices and express their opinions. The following are ideas for encouraging an open and flexible organizational structure:

1. Design strategies to provide students, parents, and the community with opportunities to comment on the school plans, procedures, and activities.

2. Include students, where appropriate, in all school committees.

3. Expand school-site councils to include community agencies.

4. Develop outreach programs to identify and include natural student and community leaders in the school decision-making process.

5. Install a school suggestion box. Give prizes or incentives for the best ideas.

6. Establish an interagency case management team for high-risk students. Include school administrators, psychologists, health professionals, counselors, and law enforcement and probation officers.

7. Develop or augment existing school-based or school-linked collaborative programs for students and families by using counseling, psychological, social, and health services agencies in the community.

8. Provide child-care options on campus for staff and students. Develop a child-care and parenting curriculum to teach family-life skills to students who volunteer in the child-care center.

9. Ask the school board to proclaim a Safe Schools Week. (National Safe Schools Week occurs annually, the third week in October.)

Classroom Organization and Structure

A positive perception by teachers and students about the safety and comfort of the classroom is essential to a safe school. In classrooms the focus should be on learning and positive interactions between the instructor and students. A majority of the time should be devoted to learning activities, and disruptions should be minimal so that students can experience respect for themselves and others. Students at all levels of ability should have opportunities to interact through cooperative learning experiences. (See Appendix B for information on the correlation between school safety and the rest of the curriculum.)

Another major contributor to school success is a student's healthy, positive self-concept; students with well-developed social skills have a more successful school experience than do students with poor skills. Therefore, when schools and teachers place a priority on developing personal and social skills in students, they are simultaneously taking steps to ensure the students' safety, security, and success in school.

Actions such as the following will contribute to the effectiveness of the classroom environment:

1. Integrate students of all academic levels whenever possible.

2. Use cooperative learning strategies. Give teachers training on how to make positive self-esteem a primary classroom objective.

3. Incorporate curriculum components that address self-awareness, self-esteem, personal development, cultural competence, decision-making skills, civic responsibility, social relationships, and conflict management and anger control. (See Appendix B for charts showing major curriculum strands.)

4. Ensure that the curriculum is designed to accommodate different learning styles.

5. Develop peer counseling, peer advising, and conflict resolution programs to handle student conflicts.

6. Involve senior students in classroom management procedures.

Our Children Are Our Future

I have met extraordinarily wonderful people all across this nation. I have talked to students in schools, to ex-gang members, to young men in detention. I have learned so much from them. And I think that our children are our future, and we must make a strong and vigorous investment in our children and their opportunity to grow as strong, constructive human beings. But all of us, including the children of America, have a responsibility to be accountable and to be responsible.

—Janet Reno, U.S. Attorney General, in a speech to Eastern Senior High School, Washington, D.C., November, 1993

7. Encourage parents' participation in class activities.

8. Provide a means for teachers to communicate immediately with the office, when necessary.

9. Require regular homework assignments to reinforce learning opportunities.

10. Develop alternative classroom settings, such as storefronts or business settings, for high-risk students.

11. Decrease class size whenever possible.

12. Apply a campuswide discipline policy in all classrooms.

Discipline and Consequences

A school that has clearly communicated its behavioral and academic expectations must make the consequences of violating those rules known and understood by all. Rules should be realistic, practical, and relevant to the culture of the students and staff. All violations of rules must be fairly and consistently addressed, using the consequences outlined in the student handbook or other schoolwide communication. Even in safe schools, violations of rules *will* occur because students go through natural developmental stages in which they openly express rebellion and disenchantment with adult guidance. What distinguishes a safe school from an unsafe school is not that the students never violate the rules, but that the staff is fair and consistent in handling violations. The following ideas illustrate ways in which schools can communicate the rules and apply the consequences of violating the rules:

1. Involve students and parents in the development of school rules so that everyone accepts and has a sense of ownership of the rules.

2. Use checklists to be sure that school rules and procedures are consistent with state, school district, and school-site policies.

3. Ask the school district governing board to approve rules and procedures of discipline for each school in the district (*Education Code* Section 35291). Give each student a copy at enrollment and require that parents sign it to acknowledge that they have read the rules. Post the rules prominently in every classroom.

4. Be fair and consistent in enforcing the school rules.

5. Ensure that staff are familiar with the regulations for students with special needs so that disciplinary procedures do not conflict with the IEP or procedural rights of those students.

6. Create problem-solving practices, such as peer counseling programs, conflict resolution teams, class meetings, and student courts, to make discipline a developmental process, rather than merely a punitive reaction.

7. Establish an ombudsman program so that students and staff have alternatives when they feel a misunderstanding has occurred.

8. Meet with students periodically to review school rules and consequences.

9. Require each teacher to have a specific discipline plan for the classroom and to communicate it to students, parents, and administration.

10. Provide in-service training for all certificated and noncertificated staff in managing discipline problems and communicate the expectation that all staff are responsible for responding to problems in a constructive and effective manner.

11. Teach staff how to de-escalate potentially volatile situations at school, handle combatants, project a calm appearance, and deal with bystanders' behavior.

12. Alert parents immediately to problems of attendance. Respond promptly to students who are truant or who are having academic or behavioral difficulties. Refer them to the school-site committee or the School Attendance Review Board, when warranted.

13. Follow statutory requirements for suspension and expulsion. Train all teachers and administrators about their rights and responsibilities in suspension and expulsion procedures.

The Placer County Office of Education, in collaboration with the Placer County Superior Court, district attorney, public defender, probation department, and local high school districts, is implementing a juvenile justice program that includes a peer court. The program objectives include the following:

1. Develop and implement a program that will teach students their rights and responsibilities under the juvenile justice system.

2. Establish a peer court in which youths who have committed low-level offenses will be sentenced by a jury of their peers.

3. Involve the police and sheriff departments, probation officers, district attorney, public defender, juvenile court judges, and schools in a collaborative effort to address the increasing number of juvenile offenders.

4. Develop a curriculum on juvenile laws, rights, and responsibilities to be taught at the ninth grade level.

5. Provide in-service training for teachers who integrate the unit into their curriculum.

6. In cooperation with law enforcement officials and attorneys, train students to participate as court staff—bailiff, clerk, attorney, and so forth—in presenting cases before a teen jury.

7. Prepare high school students to sit as jury members and determine fair sentences for youths who have committed low-level offenses.

8. Provide a diversion program to help reduce recidivism.

9. Increase the effectiveness of school/law enforcement partnerships by creating positive programs for students.

10. Provide positive role models and one-on-one counseling for defendants who come before the peer court.

11. Provide an opportunity for defendants to see the other side of the law by participating in a peer court jury. As a condition of sentencing, require each offender to serve two terms as a juror.

12. Create an advisory board composed of representatives from the school, probation department, juvenile justice and delinquency prevention commission, district attorney's office, public defender's office, and superior court.

For more information, contact Placer County Peer Court, Placer County Office of Education, 360 Nevada Street, Auburn, CA 95603; telephone (916) 663-4556.

Provide specialized training for those staff members responsible for carrying out attendance severance and transfer procedures so that they follow due-process requirements. Provide a legal advisor for questions about appropriate actions.

14. Develop an information management system to keep track of disciplinary incidents. Be sure to forward the discipline files of suspended or expelled students to new school districts if the students change schools. This documentation is necessary if the other school wishes to deny entrance for disciplinary reasons. Hold hearings before admitting such students.

15. Establish a policy of holding students and their parents financially accountable for destruction of school property and rewards that are paid.

16. Encourage teachers to require that suspended students return to school with all homework assignments completed.

17. Maintain an in-school suspension center that students must attend to serve suspension time.

18. Offer positive alternatives to suspension, such as participation in school beautification work projects.

19. Make clear distinctions between disciplinary issues and criminal infractions. Establish policies and procedures to report all criminal behavior to law enforcement agencies.

20. Establish clear policies for searches, seizures, handling of intruders, and responses to assaultive behavior and discovery of drugs or weapons on campus.

21. Familiarize law enforcement officials with school rules, procedures, bell schedules, and off-campus permits so that they may help enforce the school rules, policies, and procedures in the community.

22. Communicate regularly with juvenile court and probation department staff about students who are on probation.

23. Conduct truancy sweeps in association with law enforcement agencies and probation departments to return students to school. Refer students who are habitually truant to SARB or truancy mediation programs (EC § 48260.6). If the problem is not resolved, refer the student to the probation department for juvenile court processing or refer the parent to the district attorney for adult court action.

Parents' Liability

Parents can be held financially liable when their child's willful misconduct results in personal injury or destruction of school property. Provisions in California law set these current liability limits for parents:

- $10,000 for personal or property damage; adjusted yearly (EC § 48904[a][1])

- $10,000 for reward (GC § 53069.5 and EC § 48904[a][1]).

- $10,000 for personal or property damage (CC § 1714.1)

- Up to $30,000 for personal or property damage involving use of firearms (CC § 1714.3)

Participation and Involvement

Safe schools are ones that solicit the active involvement of students, teachers, and parents in decision making. This involvement creates a sense of ownership, which, in turn, engenders a spirit of concern about the direction of the school. The following strategies will encourage participation and involvement in the school:

1. Develop or enhance parent-teacher group participation. Hold some meetings at breakfast or lunch times to encourage the participation of working parents.

2. Involve the School Site Council in all stages of decision making.

3. Promote student responsibility for safer schools.

4. Encourage staff to contact parents personally on a regular basis.

5. Solicit feedback from recent graduates about school safety issues.

6. Develop a list of school, district, county, and community resource people to assist with safety issues.

7. Include safety information "windows" in student, parent, and faculty newsletters or memos.

8. Conduct a public relations campaign about the school's safety efforts. Advertise school events on marquees or billboards to encourage community participation. Set up school information booths at community events. Send public service announcements to local media about school safety issues and programs. Encourage media coverage of school activities and accomplishments.

9. Publish a school safety brochure for distribution throughout the community. Update the brochure regularly with facts about school and district safety.

10. Identify community agencies that serve youths and enlist their assis-

Parents on Campus

The goal of the *Parents on Campus* program is to promote quality education for all students by creating a safe, stable, and conducive learning environment on their campus. This feat is accomplished through active parental involvement and participation at the school four hours a day. Since its implementation there have been positive changes in both the attitudes and atmosphere on the John F. Kennedy High School campus as well as a reduction in school violence. The success of this program is simple. Concerned parents got involved and showed that they cared. This can be seen and felt through their dedication and commitment to be on campus daily for their students.

—Pam Broadfoot, Chairperson
Parents on Campus, Sacramento

tance in setting up prevention and intervention activities.

11. Work with the local parks and recreation department to develop after-school recreation programs.

12. Promote Adopt-a-School, mentors for at-risk students, tutoring, incentive, and other partnership programs for adoption by community businesses.

13. Create or strengthen your SARB. Circulate names and telephone lists of members. Consider publishing statistics on SARB cases.

14. Work closely and cooperatively with law enforcement agencies. Alert them to conditions or trends that concern you.

15. Establish an Officer Friendly program or hire a school resource officer.

16. Set up student and staff ride-alongs with law enforcement officers.

17. Participate in the National Safe Schools Week, held annually during the third week of October.

18. Emphasize the effectiveness of interagency systems. Be knowledgeable about agreements that already exist. Establish a strong, supportive network with managers in the other agencies.

19. Routinely invite governmental representatives to school functions.

20. Establish a parent telephone network to publicize school safety events or to increase parents' attendance at school functions.

21. Involve the juvenile court judge in safe school issues. Invite the judge to lunch on campus. Ask him or her to ensure that the schools are receiving mandatory records of juvenile court proceedings involving serious violence or drugs (see Appendix E). Obtain court orders to allow easy information sharing between juvenile justice agencies and the schools to better monitor students who are involved in criminal activity. For example, juvenile justice agencies can inform schools about the terms and conditions of probation and the names of students' probation officers. Schools can inform the courts about students' academic, attendance, and behavior records.

22. Ask juvenile justice providers to meet with the school safety team semi-annually to evaluate statistics on school crime reports, expulsion and suspension summaries, child abuse reports, local crime reports, and significant work order reports for maintenance related to vandalism. Use the information to evaluate needs and staffing and to create action plans.

23. Issue "Golden Apple" cards to senior citizens, providing complimentary or reduced admission to school events.

Strategies and Actions for Component 4

The following suggestions relate to the *school's culture*.

Affiliation and Bonding

The relative safety of a school is proportionate to the percentage of students and staff who can say, "This is *our* school." In safe schools students and staff believe that each individual is committed to the welfare of the others. A safe school will emphasize a norm that supports the respect and dignity of each person. In such schools the ethnic, cultural, and religious backgrounds of students will be acknowledged and respected; and incidents of students being ridiculed and isolated from the mainstream school culture will be rare. Many programs and strategies will be in place to encourage and support the interpersonal involvement among students and staff; to encourage a belief that they are safe (physically, socially, and psychologically); to build resiliency factors (see Appendix C); and to emphasize that others at school will support them in times of need. Activities that foster affiliation and bonding are as follows:

1. Conduct student attitude surveys and publish the results in school newspapers.

2. Develop a buddy system for the orientation of new students.

A Community Approach: The San Bernardino County Children's Network

Like children's networks in other communities, the Children's Network of San Bernardino County concerns itself with *children at risk.* The network consists of a variety of public and private agencies that provide direct services to those children. The goal of the network is to improve communications, planning, coordination, and cooperation among agencies serving youths; identify gaps and overlaps in services; provide a forum for clarifying perceptions and expectations among agencies and between agencies and the community; set priorities for interagency projects; and implement collaborative programs, both public and private, to better serve children and youths.

The children at risk are those who are defined as minors and who, because of behavior, abuse, neglect, medical needs, educational assessment, or a detrimental daily living situation, are eligible for services from one or more of the constituent agencies of the Children's Network.

The Children's Network has six components:

- *The Children's Policy Council* is composed of department heads of county agencies that provide services to children, two members of the Board of Supervisors, the County Administrative Officer, and the Presiding Judge of the Juvenile Court.

- *The Children's Advocate Council* is a countywide council of councils composed of representatives of all advisory boards, councils, task forces, and multidisciplinary teams that are related in some way to children's services.

- *The Children's Services Team* is an interagency, mid-management problem-solving group that reviews policies and procedures related to specific projects.

- *The Children's Fund* is a nonprofit corporation that develops a public-private partnership to acquire goods and services for children who cannot obtain them through existing public or private programs.

- *The Children's Lobby* is an interagency group of legislative analysts who review child-related legislation and make recommendations to the policy council.

- *The Child Care and Development Planning Council* is responsible for developing (1) a countywide plan that sets the priorities for the use of federal child-care block grant funds in the county for children of eligible families; and (2) a comprehensive countywide, long-range plan for child-care and developmental services.

For more information, contact the San Bernardino County Children's Network, 401 North Arrowhead Avenue, Lower Level, San Bernardino, CA 92415-0040; telephone (909) 387-8966.

3. Prominently display student achievements and arts and crafts projects in community locations, such as banks, businesses, chambers of commerce, hospitals, and airports.

4. Begin a Big Student–Little Student project to bring high school students to middle schools and elementary schools to work with younger students. High school students can offer tutoring in academics, advise younger students on ways to avoid being the victims of bullies or other violence, and provide information on making the transition from elementary school to middle school and middle school to high school.

5. Encourage each class to develop a special and unique project for the school.

6. Organize lunch activities that promote positive school community feelings.

7. Promote the feeling among students and staff that "We are a family."

8. Develop partnerships with area businesses, agencies, clubs, and individu-

als to pair caring adults with at-risk students for tutoring, mentoring, and support.

9. Sponsor a "Generations Night" open house and invite students to bring as many family members as possible to school. Set up tours of the school and arrange for a photographer to take family photographs for subsequent display.

10. Teach students that reporting concerns to staff is appropriate behavior that is not tattling or "narking."

11. Do not tolerate gang activity or symbolism on campus. Maintain the school as a neutral zone that belongs to everyone.

Behavioral Expectations

Research shows that students need and appreciate having clear and consistent expectations for their behavior. Safe schools model high moral standards, send positive messages to the students, and show that the school community expects the best effort and performance of everyone. The following are a few strategies that serve to communicate behavioral expectations:

1. In staff meetings and other communications, reinforce the expectation that adults will model positive, respectful behavior toward students.

2. Develop recognition programs to honor positive student contributions and a team spirit.

3. Encourage "service learning" projects as a way of teaching cooperative, positive behavior toward others.

4. Establish clear rules for behavior; include reference to the use of radios,

Safe School Guarantee

If we expect educators to teach to higher standards and students to reach those higher standards, we must guarantee a safe, peaceful, and welcoming educational environment so that teaching and learning can flourish.

—*Delaine Eastin*
State Superintendent of
Public Instruction

skateboards, and other personal equipment at school. Emphasize that the school does not tolerate fighting, assaults, foul language, drugs, or disruptions.

5. Outlaw gang symbols and clothing at school. Maintain the campus as a neutral zone. Ask law enforcement officers to train staff in gang suppression activities.

6. Encourage students to sign contracts that they will say no to truancy, drugs, and alcohol.

7. Make students and staff aware of their rights and responsibilities.

8. Develop a student attendance improvement program.

Academic Expectations

Safe school environments communicate that they are places in which students have a chance to set their lives on a positive course—that it is desirable for individuals, and expected of them, to use their talents to succeed. In such schools everyone understands that learning and productivity are valued and that teachers expect each student to succeed. Clear and positive academic expectations help make the school environment safe by decreasing the anxiety that occurs when academic standards are vague. Clear expectations allow students and teachers to focus on the task of learning rather than debate the extent of academic expectations. Safe schools are those that respect the various learning styles of students and the differing talents that they bring to the school. Such schools communicate that they value the success of all students, not just those with strong academic or physical talents.

Creating and Reinforcing Positive Behavior

Deal with students who are gang members in the same manner you deal with other students. Reinforce positive behavior, cooperation, and self-responsibility and apply consequences to threatening antisocial or disruptive actions to reduce the attractiveness of such behavior.

— *From* On Alert! Gang Prevention: School In-Service Guidelines

The following strategies help communicate strong academic expectations:

1. Establish a policy that all students are to sign contracts stating that they will complete their homework every day.

2. Emphasize that all students can learn and that the staff expects their best efforts. Establish various forms of assistance to support and encourage learning.

3. Establish a cross-age tutoring program for students who need extra help with their work. Set aside a classroom in which students can receive help throughout the school day. Staff the classroom with trained peer tutors, older students, parents, and senior citizens. Make sure that students who have fallen behind in course work spend part of each day in the tutoring classroom.

4. Ensure that the curriculum is designed to meet the diverse learning styles of all students.

5. Make mastery of a curriculum essential for grade-level promotion.

6. Regularly inform students and parents or guardians about course and graduation requirements.

7. Develop strategies and programs to enable students to identify and enhance their diverse learning styles and special talents.

8. Through staff training and school policies, ensure that the school values the success of all students, not just those with strong academic or physical talents.

Support and Recognition

Safe schools encourage everyone to participate. In addition, the school makes every effort to publicly reward constructive, positive behavior and makes the rewards varied and personal. The following ideas illustrate potential activities for recognizing and supporting students and staff:

1. Develop a recognition process for students and staff that highlights their contributions to the school environment. Examples include Student of the Month, Teacher of the Month, and Outstanding Principal awards.

2. Honor all students, parents, and citizen volunteers with a luncheon or similar event.

3. Call parents at home or at work or send a brief note to inform them about their children's accomplishments.

4. Display students' artwork and academic achievements prominently throughout the school.

5. Use noon dances, campus lunches, donated prizes, and other reinforcements to encourage regular attendance.

6. Encourage the district to provide employment incentives to staff for regular attendance and to return cost savings on substitutes to the school.

7. Establish support groups, such as peer counseling programs for students. Design standard procedures for responding to student crises, such as child abuse, suicide, pregnancy, AIDS, crime victimization, or loss of a loved one.

8. Reward staff regularly for curriculum innovations and improvements.

Conclusion

Unfortunately, there are no silver bullets to eliminate school crime. None of the strategies suggested in this book, if taken in isolation or implemented without a planning team, will result in success. Experience shows that the success of the plan depends on the team's ability to forge a common vision—one that builds the resiliency and enhances the positive potential of every student—and to work collectively toward achieving the vision.

Think of the ideas presented in this handbook as *tools* in your *toolbox*. Many different strategies will be needed, depending on events, locale, population, and timing. Every safe school planning team will need to assess its current situation, then sort through this toolbox to see which tools are needed to create its vision. Most likely your team will discover or create new tools of its own to address unique situations.

When selecting activities to implement the plan, each committee should cross-check to ensure that it has covered all aspects of school life, including curriculum, social events, family services, and crisis response procedures. All programs in the school should be supportive of and, if possible, involved with the safe school plan.

The video *Safe Schools: A Guide for Action* was created to help you motivate your community to join in the process of creating safe schools. The video is narrated by Pat Morita, star of the *Karate Kid* movies, and includes many motivating comments from students, administrators, teachers, parents, and law enforcement personnel.

Each member of the community is important to the safe school planning effort and must become a member of the school–community safety team. If all the players are not involved, the school will not be able to deal with crime in and around the school campus. The participation of students, staff, and the community in the process of developing a safe school plan will help to ensure that the plan will have broad support. That will give the school the maximum chance to succeed in creating a positive learning environment that the entire community supports and enjoys.

 Creating Safe Schools

The process depends on *you*. So *you* talk about it. *You* make it happen. More than ever we want, we need, we have to have safe schools!

— *Pat Morita*
Safe Schools: A Guide for Action *(video)*

Appendixes

Appendix A

California State Board of Education Policy on School Safety, Discipline, and Attendance

It is the policy of the State Board of Education that all students enrolled in public schools in California have the right to attend campuses which are safe and secure. The Board believes that students cannot benefit fully from an educational program unless they attend school regularly in a school environment which is free from physical and psychological harm. The Board also believes that the leadership in providing safe schools, establishing behavior standards, and improving student attendance must come primarily from school district governing boards and superintendents. This leadership must be continuous; it must support comprehensive efforts at each school site that assist students in becoming self-directed and responsible for their own behavior.

It is further the policy of the State Board of Education that the substantial benefit students will derive from regular attendance in a safe and orderly school environment justifies a high priority and commitment of personnel and fiscal resources by the California Department of Education and by local educational agencies.

The Board believes that a beginning step toward safer schools is the development of a comprehensive plan for school safety by every public school and district in the state. The plan should be developed and integrated into the ongoing school planning efforts that currently exist and should be reviewed and updated on a regular basis. There should be a district-wide statement of philosophy, an enabling policy, and guidelines that serve as a foundation for safe school plans created by individual schools. The statement must provide a clear sense of purpose and exemplify district support for the entire planning process. The Board acknowledges that a student's academic achievement is a great deterrent to school violence; hence, a comprehensive plan should include a focus on high expectations of student performance and behavior in all aspects of the school experience.

The Board intends that safe school plans be developed cooperatively by parents, students, teachers, administrators, counselors, and community agencies, including local law enforcement, and approved by the local school district governing board. The Board also intends for school districts to establish working and collaborative relationships with law enforcement agencies, service agencies, and parents, which will provide safe and orderly schools, improve attendance, and expand services to students and parents.

The Board believes that if a comprehensive program for school safety is to have long-lasting effects, it should include a planned sequence of strategies and activities appropriate for all students and should be based on specific needs identified by a broad-based safe school committee. The program should have a major focus that is preventive in nature, but it also should include provisions to deal with immediate problems, such as truancy; racial conflict; gang activities on campus; violent behaviors; weapons possession on campus; drug, alcohol, and other substance abuse; and natural disasters. The plan should also incorporate after-school programs and extracurricular activities that address individual student needs to belong and to be respected and appreciated. Finally, the plan should include procedures for accommodating the socially inappropriate behaviors of children and youths with disabilities.

The Board believes that comprehensive safe school plans and programs should focus attention on the traits and experiences that students, teachers, administrators, and other school personnel bring to the school campus; the physical setting and conditions in which education takes place; the organizational and interpersonal processes that occur in and around the school; and the general atmosphere or spirit of the school.

Implementation of comprehensive plans and programs should provide a positive learning environment which results in the following outcomes:

- Appropriate rules, regulations, and discipline policies that are well publicized, consistently enforced, nondiscriminatory, and take into consideration the due process entitled to all students, including those with disabilities.
- Appropriate staff development that emphasizes the importance of treating students, parents, and co-workers respectfully.
- A rigorous curriculum that sets high expectations for all students' performances in academic and other subject areas.

- Effective counseling and guidance services that include personal counseling, peer programs, educational counseling, career planning, and training in job-seeking and work-related social skills.
- Supplemental and alternative instructional strategies and learning programs, including cocurricular and extracurricular activities, independent study, work experience, and alternative schools, all of which are designed to empower students to complete high school and to transfer successfully to employment or postsecondary education.
- Student handbooks that explain codes of conduct, including information on such topics as student rights and responsibilities, unacceptable behavior, and procedures for due process and appeals.
- Plans for dealing with potential disruptive conflict situations, including procedures for referrals to law enforcement agencies for serious offenses.
- Processes for continually examining the factors in school life that influence behavior and modifying those factors based on research that bring about desired behavior.
- Programs that develop a student's self-esteem, personal and social responsibility, character, and ability to resolve conflict in a pro-social manner.
- Appropriate staff development activities teaching safe school strategies, current laws affecting school safety, and crisis responses.
- Collaboration and cooperation among community agencies, law enforcement agencies, neighborhoods, parents, and schools that lead to increased school safety.
- A system of referrals to appropriate agencies for personal services needed that schools cannot provide.

Local plans for safe schools should be based on the following elements:

1. Collaborative relationships among community agencies, parents, local law enforcement agencies, and the school that lead to a common vision of a safe school and commitment to programmatic goals developed by a broad-based safe schools committee.

2. A districtwide statement of philosophy, an enabling policy, and guidelines that serve as a foundation for safe school plans created by individual schools, provide a clear sense of purpose, and exemplify district support for the entire planning process.

3. An assessment of the incidence of campus violence and vandalism, student behavior referrals resulting in suspensions or expulsions, and students' attendance patterns, including actual attendance, number of excused and unexcused absences, and reasons for nonattendance.

4. Identification of appropriate and comprehensive strategies and programs that will provide or maintain a high level of school safety.

5. A discipline policy that clearly defines expected behavior and provides consequences for deviations from the expected behavior and distinguishes discipline problems from law enforcement problems. The discipline policy should provide details on the following:

   • Rights and responsibilities of students;

   • Student code of conduct;

   • Description of specific disruptive behaviors which interfere with the classroom learning environment, such as antisocial behaviors, gang-related attire and conduct, tardiness, excessive absences, and logical consequences for the disruptive behavior;

   • Provisions for appeals, hearings, and grievances; and

   • Processes for reviewing the individual education plan of a child with disabilities before punitive action for socially inappropriate behavior is initiated.

6. Objectives and strategies to improve school safety, attendance, student behavior, and disciplinary practices and thereby reduce campus violence and provide a positive learning environment.

7. An evaluation of the effectiveness of the designated strategies in reaching the desired attendance, behavior, and school environment goals.

8. A description of the roles and responsibilities of teachers, administrators, counselors, paraprofessionals, and other school personnel in developing cooperative working relationships with law enforcement agencies, service agencies, parents, and students to assure the implementation and continuing progress of the comprehensive plan.

9. A description of the identified fiscal and personnel resources for the plan's implementation.

10. Strategies for recognizing situations that may potentially result in disruptive conflict and for implementing appropriate interventions.

(Adopted 10/21/83; revised 9/10/93)

Appendix B

Charts Showing the Correlation Between Safe School Planning, the Curriculum Frameworks, and Grade-Span Reform Initiatives

Chart 1

Correlation Between Safe School Planning and *English–Language Arts Framework* (1987)

Components of Safe School Planning	*Goal:* To prepare all students to function as informed and effective citizens in this democratic society	*Goal:* To prepare all students to function effectively in the work setting	*Goal:* To prepare all students to realize personal fulfillment	Integrate reading, discussion, writing, thinking, listening.	Establish a literature-based program	Use core literary works from all cultures and times.	Recommend extended works.	Use recreational/motivational reading.	Learn to read by reading.	Help students develop composition skills.	Develop oral language skills.
1. Personal Characteristics of Students and Staff											
• Ethnic/cultural diversity	•	•	•	•	•	•	•	•	•	•	•
• Life experiences	•	•	•	•	•	•	•	•	•	•	•
• Staff expertise/diversity	•	•	•	•	•	•					•
• Physical/health concerns	•	•	•	•	•	•	•	•	•	•	•
2. School's Physical Environment											
• School location				•	•	•	•	•			•
• School grounds								•	•		
• Buildings/classrooms				•					•		•
• Internal security procedures											
3. School's Social Environment											
• Leadership	•	•	•	•	•	•	•	•	•	•	•
• Site management	•	•	•	•	•	•	•	•	•	•	•
• Classroom organization and structure	•	•	•	•	•	•	•	•	•	•	
• Discipline and consequences	•	•	•	•	•	•	•	•	•	•	•
• Participation and involvement	•	•	•	•	•	•	•	•	•	•	•
4. School's Culture											
• Affiliation and bonding	•	•	•	•	•				•	•	•
• Behavioral expectations	•	•	•	•	•		•		•	•	•
• Academic expectations	•	•	•	•	•	•	•	•	•	•	•
• Support and recognition	•	•	•	•	•		•	•		•	•

Chart 2

Correlation Between Safe School Planning and *Foreign Language Framework* (1989)

Components of Safe School Planning	Teaching and learning are *in* the language, not about the language.	Language is studied in its cultural context.	Model curriculum includes instruction in European, Pacific Rim, classical, and sign languages, ESL, and native languages for non-English speakers.	Program includes time for reviewing, planning, and implementing improvements.	Program includes appropriate instruction in the classroom and beyond.	Program is articulated—K through grade twelve.	Program is integrated with rest of curriculum.	Student evaluation is based on communication skills.	Instruction makes use of technology and media aids, realia, and printed materials.	Program receives support from district, business, and community.	Students learn to function well enough in English to be successful in programs for native English speakers.
1. Personal Characteristics of Students and Staff											
• Ethnic/cultural diversity	●	●	●		●						●
• Life experiences	●	●	●								
• Staff expertise/diversity	●	●	●	●	●	●	●	●	●	●	●
• Physical/health concerns	●							●			●
2. School's Physical Environment											
• School location		●									
• School grounds											
• Buildings/classrooms		●	●		●	●	●	●	●	●	
• Internal security procedures											
3. School's Social Environment											
• Leadership		●	●	●	●	●	●		●	●	●
• Site management			●	●	●	●	●			●	
• Classroom organization and structure	●	●	●	●	●	●	●	●	●	●	●
• Discipline and consequences								●			
• Participation and involvement	●	●	●	●	●	●	●		●	●	●
4. School's Culture											
• Affiliation and bonding	●	●	●	●	●	●	●	●	●	●	●
• Behavioral expectations	●	●		●	●			●			●
• Academic expectations	●	●	●	●	●	●	●	●	●		●
• Support and recognition	●	●	●	●	●	●	●	●	●	●	●

Chart 3

Correlation Between Safe School Planning and *Health Framework* (1994)

Components of Safe School Planning	Acceptance of personal responsibility for lifelong health	Respect for and promotion of the health of others	Understanding of the process of growth and development	Informed use of health-related information, products, services	Personal health	Consumer and community health	Injury prevention and safety	Alcohol, tobacco, and other drugs	Nutrition	Environmental health	Individual growth and development	Family living	Communicable and chronic diseases
1. Personal Characteristics of Students and Staff													
• Ethnic/cultural diversity		●	●		●								
• Life experiences	●	●	●		●	●		●	●	●	●	●	●
• Staff expertise/diversity													
• Physical/health concerns	●	●	●	●	●	●		●	●	●	●	●	●
2. School's Physical Environment													
• School location						●	●		●	●			
• School grounds							●	●		●			
• Buildings/classrooms		●					●			●			●
• Internal security procedures		●					●	●		●			●
3. School's Social Environment													
• Leadership		●				●	●	●		●	●	●	
• Site management							●	●		●	●	●	●
• Classroom organization and structure		●					●				●		●
• Discipline and consequences	●	●			●		●	●		●	●	●	
• Participation and involvement	●	●			●	●	●	●		●	●	●	●
4. School's Culture													
• Affiliation and bonding	●	●	●		●	●	●	●		●	●	●	●
• Behavioral expectations		●			●	●	●	●		●	●	●	●
• Academic expectations			●					●	●		●	●	●
• Support and recognition	●	●			●	●			●		●		●

Chart 4

Correlation Between Safe School Planning and *History–Social Science Framework* (1988)

Components of Safe School Planning	*Goal:* Knowledge and cultural understanding	Historical literacy	Ethical literacy	Cultural literacy	Geographic literacy	Socio-political literacy	*Goal:* Democratic understanding and civic values	National identity	Constitutional heritage	Civic values, rights, responsibilities	*Goal:* Skill attainment and social participation	Participation skills	Critical thinking skills	Basic study skills
1. Personal Characteristics of Students and Staff														
• Ethnic/cultural diversity	•			•	•	•		•			•		•	•
• Life experiences		•	•	•	•	•		•			•		•	•
• Staff expertise/diversity	•			•							•			
• Physical/health concerns														
2. School's Physical Environment														
• School location				•	•	•								
• School grounds														
• Buildings/classrooms											•			
• Internal security procedures											•			
3. School's Social Environment														
• Leadership	•		•	•		•				•	•	•	•	•
• Site management				•		•					•	•	•	•
• Classroom organization and structure	•			•		•				•	•	•	•	•
• Discipline and consequences			•						•	•	•	•		
• Participation and involvement	•		•	•		•				•	•	•	•	
4. School's Culture														
• Affiliation and bonding	•			•	•			•		•	•		•	
• Behavioral expectations			•						•	•	•			
• Academic expectations			•								•		•	•
• Support and recognition	•			•							•	•		

Chart 5

Correlation Between Safe School Planning and *Mathematics Framework* (1992)

Components of Safe School Planning	Students will learn basic computational techniques.	Students will learn problem-solving techniques.	Students will learn investigation techniques.	Students will learn mathematical thinking.	Students will learn mathematical communication.	Students will learn about mathematical tools and ideas.	Students will learn to work independently and collaboratively.	Mathematics will be connected to history and science.	Students will be expected to complete quality work.	Students are given tasks worthy of quality, large-scale work.	Instruction uses books, manipulatives, technology.	*All* students participate fully.	Students take responsibility for their learning.	Instruction is not biased by race, gender, or culture.
1. Personal Characteristics of Students and Staff														
• Ethnic/cultural diversity							•					•	•	•
• Life experiences		•					•			•		•	•	•
• Staff expertise/diversity	•		•	•	•	•	•	•	•	•	•	•	•	•
• Physical/health concerns									•			•	•	•
2. School's Physical Environment														
• School location														
• School grounds														
• Buildings/classrooms	•	•	•	•	•	•	•	•	•	•	•	•		•
• Internal security procedures									•			•		
3. School's Social Environment														
• Leadership				•	•	•	•	•	•	•	•	•	•	•
• Site management					•			•			•	•		•
• Classroom organization and structure	•	•	•	•	•	•		•	•	•	•	•	•	•
• Discipline and consequences	•	•	•	•	•	•	•		•			•	•	•
• Participation and involvement	•	•	•	•	•	•	•		•	•		•	•	•
4. School's Culture														
• Affiliation and bonding	•	•	•	•	•	•	•		•			•	•	•
• Behavioral expectations	•	•	•	•	•	•	•		•			•	•	•
• Academic expectations	•	•	•	•	•	•	•	•		•	•	•	•	•
• Support and recognition	•	•	•	•	•	•	•	•	•			•	•	•

Chart 6

Correlation Between Safe School Planning and *Physical Education Framework* (1994)

Components of Safe School Planning	Students will develop skills in and knowledge of movement.	Promote a positive self-image and personal development.	Promote social development.	Develop sensorimotor and perceptual motor skills (kinesthetic, visual, tactile, auditory).	Develop locomotor skills (walking, running, skipping, hopping).	Develop nonlocomotor skills (bending, pushing, and so forth).	Develop balance.	Develop hand-eye coordination (throwing, catching, pouring, cutting).	Develop eye-foot coordination (kicking, trapping, dribbling, punting).	Develop general coordination (swinging, climbing, sliding, jumping rope, tumbling).	Develop creative movement skills (move to music).
1. Personal Characteristics of Students and Staff											
• Ethnic/cultural diversity	●	●	●								●
• Life experiences		●	●								●
• Staff expertise/diversity	●	●	●	●	●	●	●	●	●	●	●
• Physical/health concerns	●	●	●	●	●	●	●	●	●	●	●
2. School's Physical Environment											
• School location	●	●	●								
• School grounds	●	●	●	●	●	●	●	●	●	●	●
• Buildings/classrooms	●	●	●	●	●	●	●	●	●	●	●
• Internal security procedures	●	●	●								
3. School's Social Environment											
• Leadership		●	●								●
• Site management		●	●								
• Classroom organization and structure	●	●	●	●	●	●	●	●	●	●	●
• Discipline and consequences	●	●	●		●	●	●	●	●	●	●
• Participation and involvement	●	●	●		●	●	●	●	●	●	●
4. School's Culture											
• Affiliation and bonding	●	●	●		●	●					●
• Behavioral expectations	●	●	●		●	●	●	●	●	●	●
• Academic expectations	●	●	●								●
• Support and recognition	●	●	●		●	●	●	●	●	●	●

Chart 7

Correlation Between Safe School Planning and *Science Framework* (1990)

Components of Safe School Planning	Students will use science themes: energy, evolution, patterns of change, scale and structure, stability, systems and interactions.	Themes integrate concepts through all curricular areas.	Themes are used to improve writing skills.	Assessment is based on themes.	Students learn observation skills.	Students learn communication skills.	Students learn the skill of comparing.	Students learn to order and categorize.	Students learn to relate factors.	Students learn to infer and apply knowledge.	Students learn to make decisions about major issues.	All students participate in discussions and cooperative learning.	Students learn scientific ethics and values.
1. Personal Characteristics of Students and Staff													
• Ethnic/cultural diversity											●	●	●
• Life experiences				●							●	●	●
• Staff expertise/diversity	●	●	●	●	●	●	●	●	●	●	●	●	●
• Physical/health concerns											●	●	●
2. School's Physical Environment													
• School location													●
• School grounds					●	●	●	●	●	●	●	●	●
• Buildings/classrooms	●	●	●		●	●	●	●	●	●	●	●	●
• Internal security procedures													
3. School's Social Environment													
• Leadership		●	●		●	●	●	●	●	●	●	●	●
• Site management			●		●	●					●	●	●
• Classroom organization and structure	●	●	●	●	●	●							
• Discipline and consequences	●	●	●		●	●	●	●	●	●		●	●
• Participation and involvement	●	●	●		●	●	●	●	●	●		●	●
4. School's Culture													
• Affiliation and bonding	●	●	●		●	●					●	●	●
• Behavioral expectations	●	●	●		●	●		●	●	●	●	●	●
• Academic expectations	●	●	●	●	●	●	●	●	●	●	●	●	●
• Support and recognition	●	●	●	●	●	●	●	●	●	●	●	●	●

Chart 8

Correlation Between Safe School Planning and *Visual and Performing Arts Framework* (1989)

Components of Safe School Planning	All students develop aesthetic perception and multisensory integration in:				All students develop abilities for creative expression in:				Students learn to recognize the major themes, historical periods, and cultural expressions used in world cultures, past and present, through:				Students learn about aesthetic values for the enjoyment, observation, recognition, and aesthetic judgment of:			
	Dance	Drama/theatre	Music	Visual arts	Dance	Drama/theatre	Music	Visual arts	Dance	Drama/theatre	Music	Visual arts	Dance	Drama/theatre	Music	Visual arts
1. Personal Characteristics of Students and Staff																
• Ethnic/cultural diversity	●	●	●	●	●	●	●	●	●	●	●	●				
• Life experiences	●	●	●	●	●	●	●	●	●	●	●	●				
• Staff expertise/diversity	●	●	●	●	●	●	●	●	●	●	●	●	●	●	●	●
• Physical/health concerns	●	●	●	●	●	●	●	●	●	●	●	●	●	●	●	●
2. School's Physical Environment																
• School location																
• School grounds	●	●	●	●	●	●	●	●					●	●	●	●
• Buildings/classrooms	●	●	●	●	●	●	●	●					●	●	●	●
• Internal security procedures					●	●	●	●								
3. School's Social Environment																
• Leadership									●	●	●	●	●	●	●	●
• Site management	●	●	●	●	●	●	●	●	●	●	●	●	●	●	●	●
• Classroom organization and structure	●	●	●	●	●	●	●	●	●	●	●	●	●	●	●	●
• Discipline and consequences					●	●	●	●	●	●	●	●				
• Participation and involvement	●	●	●	●	●	●	●	●	●	●	●	●	●	●	●	●
4. School's Culture																
• Affiliation and bonding	●	●	●	●	●	●	●	●	●	●	●	●	●	●	●	●
• Behavioral expectations	●	●	●	●	●	●	●	●	●	●	●	●	●	●	●	●
• Academic expectations	●	●	●	●	●	●	●	●	●	●	●	●	●	●	●	●
• Support and recognition	●	●	●	●	●	●	●	●	●	●	●	●	●	●	●	●

Chart 9

Correlation Between Safe School Planning and *Here They Come: Ready or Not! Report of the School Readiness Task Force* (1988)

Components of Safe School Planning	Ability to use language for complex communication	Ability to recognize and use opportunities for learning through language, reading, and the arts	Ability to use problem-solving strategies	Ability to solve meaningful mathematical problems	Ability to play individually and with peers and to function as a member of a group	Ability to demonstrate self-control and self-discipline	Ability to sustain interest in an activity and listen to adults and peers	Ability to be intrinsically motivated (curious about and challenged by the world)	Development of fine and gross motor skills and coordination
1. Personal Characteristics of Students and Staff									
• Ethnic/cultural diversity	●	●	●		●	●	●	●	●
• Life experiences	●	●	●	●	●	●	●	●	●
• Staff expertise/diversity	●								
• Physical/health concerns	●				●	●	●	●	●
2. School's Physical Environment									
• School location									
• School grounds					●				●
• Buildings/classrooms					●				●
• Internal security procedures					●				●
3. School's Social Environment									
• Leadership	●	●	●		●	●			
• Site management									
• Classroom organization and structure	●	●	●	●	●	●	●	●	●
• Discipline and consequences	●	●	●		●	●	●		
• Participation and involvement	●	●	●	●	●		●		●
4. School's Culture									
• Affiliation and bonding	●	●	●		●	●	●		
• Behavioral expectations	●	●	●		●	●	●		
• Academic expectations	●	●	●	●	●	●	●	●	
• Support and recognition	●	●		●	●	●	●	●	●

Chart 10

Correlation Between Safe School Planning and *It's Elementary!* *Elementary Grades Task Force Report (1992)*

Components of Safe School Planning	Focus all instruction on a thinking curriculum.	Reduce time spent on skill-building activities.	Choose depth over breadth.	Schedule longer periods for class work.	Team teach and specialize.	Extend learning with homework.	Use a variety of grouping strategies.	Provide collaborative learning opportunities.	Intervene early to prevent learning problems.	Develop academic support networks to ensure learning.	Ensure that LEP students have access to thinking curriculum.	Avoid retention.	Recruit teachers from diverse backgrounds.	Make students feel a part of a caring community.
1. Personal Characteristics of Students and Staff														
• Ethnic/cultural diversity	●			●	●	●							●	●
• Life experiences		●		●	●	●		●			●		●	●
• Staff expertise/diversity	●			●				●			●			
• Physical/health concerns											●			
2. School's Physical Environment														
• School location				●	●	●								
• School grounds														
• Buildings/classrooms											●			
• Internal security procedures											●			
3. School's Social Environment														
• Leadership	●		●	●		●	●				●	●	●	●
• Site management				●		●	●			●	●	●	●	●
• Classroom organization and structure	●			●		●	●			●	●	●	●	●
• Discipline and consequences			●				●		●	●	●		●	
• Participation and involvement	●		●			●	●			●	●	●	●	
4. School's Culture														
• Affiliation and bonding	●			●	●		●	●		●	●	●	●	
• Behavioral expectations			●				●		●	●	●			
• Academic expectations			●								●	●	●	●
• Support and recognition	●			●							●	●		

Chart 11

Correlation Between Safe School Planning and *Caught in the Middle* (1987)

Components of Safe School Planning	Help every student develop the capacity for critical thought and effective communication.	Help all students to make moral and ethical choices.	Teach students study skills—learn how to learn.	Provide academic counseling; prepare for high school.	Ensure equal access to content mastery.	Provide support for minority students.	Provide programs to help those at risk of dropping out.	Provide guidance and health-care services.	Develop a positive, student-centered school culture.	Provide access to extracurricular and intramural activities.	Facilitate transitions from elementary to middle to high school.	Ensure that schedule allows equal access to programs.	Provide staff development to achieve goals.	Involve parents and community in plans.
1. Personal Characteristics of Students and Staff														
• Ethnic/cultural diversity	•	•			•	•	•	•	•	•	•			•
• Life experiences	•	•			•	•	•	•	•	•	•	•	•	•
• Staff expertise/diversity	•	•	•	•	•	•	•		•		•			•
• Physical/health concerns	•		•	•	•	•	•		•	•	•	•		•
2. School's Physical Environment														
• School location										•	•			•
• School grounds								•	•	•				•
• Buildings/classrooms			•						•					•
• Internal security procedures									•					
3. School's Social Environment														
• Leadership	•	•	•		•	•	•	•	•	•	•	•	•	•
• Site management		•	•	•	•	•	•	•	•	•	•	•	•	•
• Classroom organization and structure	•	•	•	•	•	•	•	•	•		•	•	•	•
• Discipline and consequences	•	•	•	•	•	•	•		•				•	
• Participation and involvement	•	•	•	•	•	•	•	•	•	•	•	•	•	•
4. School's Culture														
• Affiliation and bonding	•	•	•	•	•	•	•	•	•	•	•	•	•	•
• Behavioral expectations	•	•	•	•	•	•	•	•	•	•	•	•	•	•
• Academic expectations	•	•	•	•	•	•	•		•	•	•	•	•	•
• Support and recognition	•	•	•		•	•	•	•	•	•	•	•		•

Chart 12
Correlation Between Safe School Planning and *Second to None* (1992)

Components of Safe School Planning	Students and teachers work in clusters to support student learning.	Every student has a plan and can make choices.	Students are offered advanced learning opportunities.	Teachers are effective coaches.	Students collaborate as active learners.	Instructional material and technology are better utilized.	Student assessment is outcome-based and continuous.	Schools compile graduation portfolios.	Student support is an intrinsic part of the school.	Students receive individual attention.	School is part of a network of community services.	Enabler courses help students gain key skills and knowledge.	School is responsible for students' success.	Facilities are organized by clusters.
1. Personal Characteristics of Students and Staff														
• Ethnic/cultural diversity	●	●	●	●	●				●	●	●	●	●	●
• Life experiences	●	●	●	●	●	●			●	●	●	●	●	●
• Staff expertise/diversity	●	●	●	●	●	●	●	●	●	●	●		●	●
• Physical/health concerns	●	●	●	●	●	●			●	●	●	●	●	●
2. School's Physical Environment														
• School location			●											
• School grounds	●								●		●		●	●
• Buildings/classrooms						●			●	●	●		●	●
• Internal security procedures											●		●	
3. School's Social Environment														
• Leadership	●	●	●	●	●	●	●		●	●	●	●	●	●
• Site management	●	●	●	●	●	●	●	●	●	●	●	●	●	●
• Classroom organization and structure	●	●	●	●	●	●	●	●	●	●	●	●	●	●
• Discipline and consequences				●	●	●	●		●	●	●	●	●	
• Participation and involvement	●	●	●	●			●						●	
4. School's Culture														
• Affiliation and bonding	●	●	●	●	●		●		●	●		●	●	●
• Behavioral expectations	●	●	●	●	●		●		●	●			●	●
• Academic expectations	●	●	●	●	●	●	●	●	●	●		●	●	●
• Support and recognition	●	●	●	●	●		●	●	●	●	●	●	●	●

Appendix C

Building Resiliency in Youths and Strengthening Protective Factors

I. Resilience

Resilience can be defined as the capacity to spring back, rebound, successfully adapt in the face of adversity, and develop social competence despite exposure to severe stress.

II. Profile of Resilient Children

A. Effectiveness in work, play, and relationships
   - Establish healthy friendships.
   - Set goals.

B. Healthy expectancies and positive outlook
   - Believe that effort and initiative will pay off.
   - Are oriented to success rather than failure.

C. Self-efficacy
   - Feel competent.
   - Have an internal center of control.
   - Believe they can control events in their environment rather than be passive victims.

D. Self-discipline
   - Have the ability to delay gratification and control impulse drives.
   - Maintain an orientation to the future.

E. Critical thinking and problem-solving skills
   - Are able to think abstractly/reflectively.
   - Are flexible.

F. Sense of humor

III. Protective Factors

A. Peers
   - Respect authority.
   - Bond to conventional groups.
   - Appreciate unique contributions and talents of individuals.
   - Are involved in drug-free activities.

Source: Adapted from materials developed by the Western Center for Drug-Free Schools and Communities, in *School/Community Violence Prevention: Focus on Gangs.* Sacramento: California Department of Education and the Office of the California Attorney General, 1994.

B. Community
  • Provides access to resources (e.g., housing, health care, child care, job training, employment, recreation)
  • Supplies norms and public policies for nonuse of alcohol, tobacco, and other drugs among youths

C. School
  • Expresses high expectations
  • Encourages goal setting and self-mastery
  • Encourages staff members to view themselves as nurturing caretakers
  • Encourages pro-social development
  • Provides leadership and decision-making opportunities
  • Provides staff development opportunities in social development and cooperative learning
  • Involves parents
  • Provides positive activities that are free of alcohol, tobacco, or other drugs (involvement in alcohol, tobacco, and other drugs is often part of the gang subculture)

D. Family
  • Seeks prenatal care
  • Develops close bonding with the child
  • Values and encourages education
  • Manages stress well
  • Spends quality time with children
  • Uses a high-warmth/low-criticism parenting style
  • Sets clear expectations of children
  • Encourages supportive relationships with other significant adults
  • Shares family responsibilities

IV. **Four Basic Protective Factors for Planning**

  A. Promote the bonding of students to family, school, and positive peer groups through opportunities for active participation.

  B. Define a clear set of norms.

  C. Teach students the skills needed to live within the norms and make use of opportunities.

  D. Provide recognition, rewards, and reinforcement for newly learned skills and positive behavior.

V. **Fostering Resiliency**

  Resilience describes that quality in children who, though exposed to significant stress and adversity in their lives, do not succumb to school failure, substance abuse, mental illness, or juvenile delinquency. Researchers have asked: "What makes resilient children?" "Why do some children function in spite of their life's problems, while others have so many problems?" "What makes the difference?"

Historically, social and behavioral sciences have followed a problem-focused approach to studying human and social development. This "pathology" model of research traditionally examines problems, disease, illness, incompetence, and so forth. Emphasis has been placed on identifying risk factors of various disorders, such as alcoholism and delinquency. Longitudinal research on children growing up in situations of great stress and adversity found that although a certain percentage of high-risk children developed various problems (a percentage higher than the normal population), a greater percentage of the children became healthy, competent young adults.

How do these "at-risk" children sidestep the negative outcomes and move safely into a healthy adulthood? Over many years researchers have identified protective factors present in the children and their families, schools, and community environments. These factors foster the development of resilient attributes that, in turn, help the children successfully avoid, minimize, or overcome risks. The key protective factors are as follows:

- A caring and supportive relationship between the child and at least one person
- Consistent, clear communication of high expectations of the child
- Ample opportunities for the child to participate in and contribute meaningfully to his or her social environment.

The attributes of social competence, problem-solving skills, autonomy, and sense of purpose appear to be the common threads running through the personalities of resilient children. Resilient children are considerably more responsive and can elicit more positive responses from others; the children are more active, flexible, and adaptable. Their social competence includes a sense of humor, empathy, and caring. Research on resilient children has revealed that they have problem-solving skills that are identifiable in early childhood.

Family-like organizations and activities that foster resiliency differ in at least six crucial elements of design and orientation from those youth-serving institutions that are less successful in attracting and engaging adolescents. These organizations:

1. See youths as resources to be developed, rather than as problems to be managed.
2. Have activities that yield a recognizable product, such as a performance, newspaper, or team record.
3. Have their roots deep in the community and neighborhoods.
4. Are responsive to the local ecology, the untapped resources, and unmet needs of those who become their members.
5. Encourage ownership and trust by the young participants. (A program attractive to teenagers is a program that they feel belongs to them.)
6. Listen to and respond to the needs of the community.

People within a community have the skills to solve their problems. Public energy and money should be going into intergenerational social networks that are established to provide safety nets for young children. The clear finding from years of research into communities and neighborhoods rich in social networks is that those communities have lower rates of crime, delinquency, child abuse, and other related problems.

Appendix D

Outsiders and Other Interference

Possibly the most time-consuming and annoying criminal problem that administrators face is keeping unauthorized persons from entering the school campus. The laws restricting such persons from schools are complex, making the laws difficult for school staff and police to enforce. Most of the laws require proof that the nonstudent intends to disturb, disrupt, or interfere with school activities—an intention that is often difficult to establish (see PC §§ 626.2, 626.4, 626.6, 626.8, 627–627.10; EC § 32211). Many statutes require administrators specifically to request an intruder to leave the campus. If the intruder refuses to leave or returns within seven days of the original order to leave, he or she may be arrested for a criminal offense.

If a school has a constant problem with outsiders entering the campus or loitering around the perimeter of the campus, it is best to call a meeting with law enforcement personnel and a representative of the district attorney's office to discuss the situation. The group should agree on which trespass or disruption statute will be used to cite offenders. School staff and law enforcement staff should then be carefully trained to recognize when an offender has committed the acts necessary to bring him or her within the scope of the statute. By working together as an interagency group on a tough enforcement and prosecution program, the staff of both agencies can alleviate the frustration of dealing with school trespassers. In addition to receiving a fine or time in custody, all offenders should be placed on probation with terms and conditions that require those persons to stay away from the school. Proving a violation of the court's order is usually far simpler than proving the violation of elements of the trespass statute itself. The offender is then subject to further punishment. A strong message will be sent to those offenders that their misbehavior will no longer be tolerated.

Appendix E

Mandatory Cross-Reporting Responsibilities

Clear and specific policies and procedures must be established to address serious offenses and criminal infractions when they occur on school campuses. Interagency agreements between law enforcement agencies and schools serve to identify those circumstances that require law enforcement intervention and to detail procedures so that everyone knows what to expect.

Criminal Behavior—When to Call Law Enforcement Officials

School staff should meet with law enforcement officials to discuss crimes that typically occur on or near campus. This interagency group should work out an agreement on the kinds of crime that should be reported to law enforcement agencies. Felony crimes should always be reported. For example:

1. Possession of knives, guns, and other dangerous weapons at school is not only an offense that can result in expulsion or suspension from school but also a criminal offense (EC §§ 48915[a], 48915.1, 48902, 49330–49333; 5 CCR 3052; and PC §§ 626.9-626.10, 12020, 12025, 12031, 653[k]).
2. An assault against any person by a pupil using a deadly weapon or force likely to produce great bodily injury, resulting in the suspension or expulsion of the pupil committing the assault, shall be reported to law enforcement authorities by the school principal (EC § 48902).

3. Assaults and batteries committed on school property against any person carry higher penalties than if those crimes had occurred elsewhere (PC §§ 241.2, 243.2, 243.3, 243.5). In addition, assaults on school employees by pupils must be reported to law enforcement authorities (EC §§ 44014, 48902). An employee who is attacked, assaulted, or menaced by a pupil has a duty to report the incident to law enforcement officials. The employee's supervisor has the same responsibility. Both can be fined up to $200 if they fail to report the occurrence (EC § 44014).
4. Any use, possession, furnishing, or sale of drugs or alcohol at school should be handled with disciplinary sanctions as well as reported to law enforcement authorities. Schools with serious drug trafficking on campus should not hesitate to work closely with law enforcement officials to apprehend the offenders (EC § 48902).
5. *Education Code* Section 48902 states that schools shall, prior to the suspension or expulsion of any pupil, report to law enforcement authorities any violations of *Penal Code* Section 245 (assault with a deadly weapon) and any acts of students that involve the possession or sales of narcotics or possession of other weapons; and schools shall notify law enforcement authorities, within one school day after the suspension or expulsion of any pupil, of an act that may violate

Education Code Section 48900(c) or (d).

A pupil who repeatedly commits misdemeanor crimes should also be reported to law enforcement authorities. This action allows the juvenile justice system to deal with offenders early in their criminal careers while there is still some ability to provide effective rehabilitation. Typically, a first-time offender's case will be handled through a diversion program. Only more serious cases and chronic offenders are sent to a juvenile court judge.

When crimes are reported to police, a record of the offense can be made accessible to the juvenile justice system. A youth who is committing crimes at school is highly likely to be committing similar offenses elsewhere in the community as well. When all crimes are reported, a more complete picture of the scope of criminal activity is gained. School staff do no favors to youthful offenders or to the community by ignoring criminal behavior at school or by treating it as only a disciplinary matter.

The best way to deal with serious habitual offenders—juvenile career criminals—is through strong cooperation among school, law enforcement, prosecution, and probation agencies. Together, these agencies identify, monitor, prosecute, and jointly supervise those minors at school and in the community (W&IC §§ 500–506).

In addition, all school staff should know the law regarding searches of students. Designated staff should be trained to conduct legal searches, when necessary, of students, lockers, students' vehicles, and other areas.

Full cooperation between schools and the juvenile justice system results in safer campuses once violators realize that schools will not tolerate criminal activity.

Court Notification of Misconduct

In 1984 the Legislature provided for mandatory notification of the misconduct of minors to the appropriate school district superintendents. *Welfare and Institutions Code* Section 827(b) requires the court to notify the district superintendent, in writing, within seven days when a minor enrolled in a district school (grades one through twelve) is adjudged guilty of involvement with narcotics or a controlled substance or has committed a serious act (as defined in W&IC § 707[b]). Section 827(b) further states that the superintendent shall expeditiously transmit this information to the teacher and others who have supervisory or disciplinary responsibility for the minor. The information received is confidential and is not to be disseminated further. The information is vital for proper supervision.

Communication Between Probation Officers, Courts, and Schools

Legislation passed recently continues to enlarge the opportunity for schools to gain greater knowledge of a student's problems and legal responsibilities. For example, *Education Code* Section 48267 requires the juvenile court to inform the district superintendent when a student has been placed on probation with conditions of school attendance. The code also requires the school to inform the juvenile court and the pupil's probation officer of any absence that is a truancy within 10 days of the occurrence. It is important for a school district to develop a form to comply with the legal responsibility of informing the court that the minor may be in the community unsupervised and in violation of the terms of probation.

Required Notification to Teachers and Schools

Education Code Section 48918(j) requires the school district to record the expulsion order of a student and the reasons for the expulsion in the student's record. The district must, on request, forward that record to any school in which the student subsequently enrolls. A pupil expelled from school for any of the offenses listed in subdivision (a) of Section 48915 shall not be permitted to enroll in any other school or school district during the period of the expulsion unless the school is a county community school or a juvenile court school (EC §§ 48915.2, 48915.7). If a pupil who has been expelled for an act other than the acts described in *Education Code* Section 48915(a) has moved to another school district, the law requires that the new school district be notified of the expulsion or any pending expulsion, and the new school district is required to hold a hearing to determine whether the pupil is a threat to students or staff (EC § 48915.1). Thus a school district has the opportunity to become aware of a student who may have a tendency toward violent behavior or who is involved with drugs. This information allows a school district more effectively to place a student in an appropriate educational program, provide for adequate supervision, and ensure the safety of all other students on campus.

Education Code Section 49079 states that a school district shall inform the teacher of each pupil who has engaged in, or is reasonably suspected to have engaged in, any of the acts described in any of the subdivisions, except subdivision (h), of Section 48900. The district shall provide the teacher with the information from any records that the district maintains in its ordinary course of business, or which it receives from a law enforcement agency, regarding a pupil described in Section 49079. This information must be based on written records that the school district maintains or receives from a law enforcement agency. Beginning with the 1992-93 school year, the information must include any records received from law enforcement agencies during the previous three years, and in every subsequent year the information will be for the most recent three-year period.

An officer or employee of a school district who knowingly fails to provide information about a pupil who has engaged in, or who is reasonably suspected to have engaged in, the acts referred to in subdivision (a) is guilty of a misdemeanor, which is punishable by confinement in the county jail for a period not to exceed six months, or by a fine not to exceed one thousand dollars ($1,000), or both (EC § 49079[c]).

Provisions in the *Education Code* require a school principal or the principal's designee to notify law enforcement officials when certain acts occur on school campuses. The acts that must be reported are assault with a deadly weapon (which also leads to the suspension or expulsion of the student), weapons possession (as defined in PC §§ 626.9, 626.10), and possession or sale of a controlled substance on campus. In addition, any school employee who is assaulted by a student on school grounds is required to report the incident to law enforcement authorities. The employee's supervisor also is required to report to the appropriate authorities if she or he is aware of the incident (EC § 44014). The purpose of making these reports is to allow the courts, probation departments, law enforcement agencies, and schools to work together in preparing and providing appropriate services for students who have the potential to disrupt a safe school environment. The issue is to create a streamlined information system that avoids cumbersome procedures and facilitates the easy transfer of data.

Section 431 of the *California Code of Regulations* (CCR), Title 5, requires the governing board to designate a certificated employee as Custodian of Records. This employee has the districtwide responsibility for overseeing compliance with required record sharing. The school district Custodian of Records should verify for the school whether the school's teachers and other identified recipients are being properly informed.

Required Notification of Disciplinary Policies and Procedures

In 1986 the Legislature added to the *Education Code* sections 35291 et seq., requiring schools to develop and adopt school-site rules and procedures on discipline. Public schools must review and adopt their rules and procedures every four years, beginning on or before December 1, 1987. Schools must solicit the participation, views, and advice of a committee representing parents, teachers, school administrators, school security personnel (if any), and, for junior and senior high schools, pupils enrolled in the school. The code sections further emphasize the duty of all school employees to enforce the adopted rules and procedures. Students and parents must be notified of the rules and procedures, and a copy of the adopted rules and procedures must be filed with the superintendent of the school district. Public involvement in the development of a school's disciplinary rules and procedures is important and results in public "buy-in" to and support for a comprehensive and sound action plan. It is important to apply all disciplinary consequences evenly and fairly, without bias toward any group on campus.

Access to School Campuses

In 1984 the Legislature enacted a series of school safety bills, one of which amended the *Penal Code* sections related to the access to school premises (PC §§ 627 et seq.). In enacting the bills the Legislature acknowledged that many serious crimes of violence are committed on school grounds by persons who are neither students nor school employees and who are not authorized to be on the school grounds. Now schools must post signs at each entrance to the campus, stating the hours in which persons entering a school campus must register in the school's main office, where that office is located, directions to the office, and the need to comply with the registration requirement. The registration allows the principal to know who the outsiders on campus are and the reason for their presence and gives the principal or the principal's designee the opportunity to refuse the outsider access to school grounds. Such refusal must be based on the principal's reasonable conclusion that the presence of the outsider would interfere with the peaceful conduct of school activities or would disrupt the school, its students, its teachers, or its other employees.

Appendix F

Suspension, Expulsion, and Involuntary Transfer

According to *Education Code* sections 48900 et seq., a pupil who commits any offense related to school activities or attendance involving the following acts or offenses may be removed from his or her school setting through **suspension, expulsion,** or **involuntary transfer** to a continuation school, opportunity program, or county community school:

- **Physical injury of another person**
- **Tobacco use**
- **Extortion (or attempts)**
- **Obscene acts, profanity**
- **Hate-motivated behavior**

- **Drug or alcohol offense**
- **Weapons possession**
- **Disruption/defiance**
- **Sexual harassment**

- **Theft**
- **Robbery (or attempts)**
- **Receipt of stolen property**
- **Gang behavior**

	Suspension	Expulsion	Involuntary Transfer
Definition	Short-term removal of a pupil from ongoing instruction at a school for adjustment purposes. May be used only when other means fail to bring about proper conduct, except for specified offenses or safety concerns. Does not include reassignment to classes at the same school for the student's normal schedule, referral to an advisor, or removal from a class during the period (EC §§ 48900, 48900.5, 48910, 48915, 48925).	Long-term removal of a pupil from the school district by action of the governing board, which may suspend the expulsion with specified conditions (EC §§ 48918, 48915, 48925). For special education students, there must be a pre-expulsion IEP (*Honig v. Doe,* 484 U.S. 305 [1988]; EC § 48915.5).	Transfer of irregularly attending, truant, or disruptive pupil to a continuation school or opportunity program or class (EC §§ 48432.5, 48637).
Who must act	Principals or superintendents (or their designees), teachers (EC §§ 48900, 48910, 48911[g][i]).	Principal or superintendent (or designee) **must** recommend expulsion if pupil causes physical injury; possesses a firearm, knife, or explosive; sells drugs; or robs or extorts others. **Must** report reasons in writing if expulsion is considered inappropriate; however, a pupil in possession of a firearm *must* be expelled (EC § 48915). Board makes final decision to expel or suspend expulsion (EC § 48915).	Principal (or designee), for transfer to continuation school; district or county screening committee, for transfer to opportunity program or class or county community school (EC §§ 1980, 48432.5, 48637.1, 48637.2).

Because the governing board can deny enrollment to a pupil expelled from another school district (if the pupil poses a potential danger to others), schools should develop a system of documentation so that subsequent school sites receiving disruptive students will have the necessary information for suspension, expulsion, denial of entrance, or other necessary actions (see EC § 48915.1).

	Suspension	Expulsion	Involuntary Transfer
How long	Principals or superintendents (or their designees): 5 days per offense; may be up to 20 days/year (30 with a disciplinary transfer); balance of semester for continuation pupil, with board's approval (EC §§ 48903, 48912.5). Teacher: remainder of day and the next day from teacher's class (EC § 48910). May request parent/ guardian to attend class with student (EC § 48900.1). For special education students, there is a maximum of 10 days (*Honig v. Doe,* supra).	Until governing board permits readmission (EC §§ 48915.1, 48916). An LEA may not expel any special education pupil if the misconduct is related to the pupil's disability (*Honig v. Doe,* supra; EC § 48915.5).	Until end of the semester following the semester during which the acts leading to the transfer occurred or as specified under required placement review (EC § 48432.5).
Due-process steps	1. Conduct informal conference with pupil, referring school employee, and principal (or designee) or superintendent (EC § 48911). 2. Tell pupil reasons for discipline and allow pupil an opportunity to present his/her side (EC § 48911). 3. Contact parent/guardian by telephone and in writing (EC § 48911). 4. Report suspension to the governing board or superinten- dent, according to board policy (EC § 48911). 5. Request conference with parent/ guardian and school (EC § 48911).	1. Hearing within 30 school days of act unless governing board meets less than weekly, in which case 40 school days are allowed (EC § 48918). 2. Give pupil written notice, facts and charges, and copy of specific rule violation; advise of right to be present, have counsel, copy documents, confront and question witnesses, present evidence, and obtain a record of the hearing (EC § 48918). 3. Board determines whether pupil is expelled subsequent to board hearing or recommendation from panel or hearing officer (EC § 48918). 4. Expulsion decision must be based on substantial evidence relevant to the charges adduced at the hearing (EC § 48911). 5. Deliberation is held in closed session, but decision to expel is made public (EC § 48918). 6. Pupil must be advised that he or she may appeal to the county board of education. Due-process rules on appeal are extremely technical. County board's decision is final (EC §§ 48918– 48924).	1. Pupil and parent are notified of proposed involuntary transfer in writing. Parent/guardian/pupil may request appeal with superintendent (or designee) (EC §§ 48432.5, 48637). 2. At meeting, pupil and parent are informed of facts and reasons for transfer; they may inspect documents, question witnesses, and present their own evidence (EC §§ 48432.5, 48637). 3. Written decision must give reasons for transfer (based on EC § 48900, truancy, or irregular attendance) and notice of any review process (EC §§ 48432.5, 48637). 4. County community school requires decision by school attendance review board (EC §§ 1981.2[b], 48432.5).

Appendix G

Work Sheets, Questionnaires, and Tally Sheets

The work sheets included in this appendix are those used by safe school trainers as they guide committees through the process of safe school planning. The committee can use these work sheets without attending a training workshop; however, the more desirable procedure is to contact the School/Law Enforcement Partnership to schedule time for the committee to attend a training session together.

The questionnaires and tally sheets that follow the work sheets are additional tools to help the committee members assess conditions at their school. Note that some questionnaires have a five-point response scale to facilitate the use of optical-scanning scoring devices.

Safe School Work Sheets

1. "Determining the Climate" helps school and community team leaders assess the general readiness for change.

2. "Establishing the Committee" helps the school-community leadership team determine whether it has included all the appropriate players on its safety planning team.

3. "Creating a Mission That Reflects the Safe School Vision" may be used by committee members to record their school's mission statement and compare it with a written version of the committee's vision that was developed through brainstorming.

4. "Data Summary" helps the committee define areas of pride and areas of concern and need from the data collected with the help of questionnaires and other sources outlined in Chapter 3.

5. "Summary Sheet: Areas of Desired Change and Action" provides a format to help the committee identify areas needing improvement or change, explore possible causes of safety concerns, and record desired actions.

6. "Developing Our Goal(s)" is designed to help the committee prioritize its desired actions and record its goal(s).

7A. "Action Plan for Component 1" helps the committee summarize existing conditions and identify objectives to meet the goal as it relates to component 1. The committee can use the work sheet to describe successful outcomes for the objective, specific activities, needed resources, responsibilities, and evaluation strategies.

7B. "Action Plan for Component 2" is similar in design to Work Sheet 7A.

7C. "Action Plan for Component 3" is similar in design to Work Sheet 7A.

7D. "Action Plan for Component 4" is similar in design to Work Sheet 7A.

7E. "Sample Action Plan for Component 1" provides a model for completing Work Sheet 7A.

8. "Overall Timeline" provides a format for recording a summary of each objective and the proposed timelines for meeting the objectives. The committee can use the work sheet to review the activities and create a coordinated, comprehensive plan.

9. "Evaluating Specific Objectives" helps the committee summarize the evaluation criteria, timelines, and achievement levels from the individual action plan statements. The summary will assist the committee in evaluating the safe school plan and determining the effectiveness of each activity.

10. "Evaluating and Assessing Our Progress" is provided to assist committee members in evaluating their safe school plan and the strategies and activities that were implemented. Use of the work sheet encourages discussion on successes, failures, and ways to strengthen and revise the plan.

Safe School Questionnaires

1. "Personal Characteristics of Students and Staff" is a general questionnaire about the school and social conditions that might affect the safety climate of the school. It is to be completed by students and staff. The questionnaire is meant to provoke thoughts about the impacts of particular social concerns on the school.

2. "The School's Physical Environment: A Physical Security Survey" helps the committee assess the physical safety of the school. A careful review of the concerns raised by these questions should help the safe school committee recognize areas of vulnerability and implement appropriate strategies to improve the school's safety.

3. "Our School's Safety" (Questionnaire for Adults) is designed primarily for school staff, community agency personnel, and parents. In some instances it may be used for high school students. The content of the questions was taken directly from the school environment components discussed in Chapter 2. The questionnaire covers all components except the personal characteristics of students and staff (see questionnaire 1). Note that a five-point response scale is used to facilitate the use of optical-scanning scoring devices.

4. "Our School's Safety" (Questionnaire for Students) is modeled after questionnaire 3 (for adults). It contains fewer items, and the wording has been changed to accommodate students at the elementary and junior-high levels. If reading comprehension is a problem among the students, the questions can be read to them. In addition, the questionnaire asks students to state whether they have been victimized in the past month by school crime or have had other negative interpersonal experiences. This information is valuable to the planning process because it helps target students' concerns.

Safe School Tally Sheets

1. "Our School's Safety" (Tally Sheet for Adults). This form is provided for recording and scoring responses to the Safe School Questionnaire 3. Scores are averaged for each sub-component in three categories: the School's Physical Environment, the School's Social Environment, and the School's Culture. The procedures to score and summarize responses to the adult questionnaire are provided on the tally sheet.

2. "Our School's Safety" (Tally Sheet for Students). This form is provided to facilitate scoring of the Safe School Questionnaire 4. The scoring procedures are the same as those for the adults' questionnaire (Tally Sheet 1). In addition, the frequency with which student victimization occurs on campus should be recorded and the information summarized for all respondents. This information can be expressed as the rate per 100 students to facilitate comparisons from year to year. The student self-report of victimization provides useful information to supplement the official crime data recorded by individual schools or districts.

3. "Observation List." This list is provided to facilitate informal observations of the school environment. Eighty observable conditions and situations on a school campus are noted. The safe school committee may want to review this list to select those items it feels may warrant observation. For example, if a particular location on campus is believed to be the site of crime or disruptive behavior, then systematic observation of that location could provide a better understanding of what happens there and what the school might do to counter any negative effects.

Safe School Work Sheet 1

Determining the Climate

1. What is the attitude toward change on the school site and in the school district?

2. How do the following groups feel about school safety planning?
    - School-site personnel
    - District personnel
    - Community at large
    - Public and community agencies
    - Law enforcement agencies
    - Media representatives

3. Do you have adequate administrative support for your planning efforts?

4. What kinds of data are available to assist you in setting goals and evaluating results?

5. Brainstorm the kinds of resources that are available to assist your team in developing a safe school plan.

Next Steps to Setting the Climate

Use the following chart to record your plans.

Task	Who will do it	When to do it

Safe School Work Sheet 2

Safe School Work Sheet 2

Establishing the Committee

1. Has your team met before?

2. What working relationship do you have with the following groups?

    *   Your local law enforcement agency

    *   The business community

    *   Social service agencies

    *   Community leaders

    *   The media

3. Which of the following school or community groups are represented on your team?

____Law enforcement agencies	____Faculty
____Community organizations	____Business
____School administration	____Students
____Health and social services	____Parents
____The media	____Probation department

4. Do your committee members represent the ethnic, cultural, and economic backgrounds of all the people in your school community?

5. What barriers to participation exist for any of the groups you need on your team for effective comprehensive planning?

6. Is there someone on the committee who has access to the types of data you will need?

Next Steps to Building the Team

Use the following chart to record your plans.

Task	*Who will do it*	*When to do it*
_____	_____	_____
_____	_____	_____
_____	_____	_____
_____	_____	_____

Creating a Mission That Reflects the Safe School Vision

The school's *safe school vision* is a futuristic look at the *ideal* of what the school would look like, how students and staff would feel, and how they would behave when all programs and strategies were successfully implemented.

1. Record your school's current mission statement:

    _____

    _____

    _____

    _____

2. Describe how your school's mission statement incorporates elements of the safe school vision:

    _____

    _____

    _____

    _____

3. Note the ways in which your school's current mission statement can be changed to reflect more closely the safe school vision:

    _____

    _____

    _____

    _____

    _____

Safe School Work Sheet 4

Data Summary

Areas of Pride and Strength	What Do We Want to Change?
Component 1:	Component 1:
Component 2:	Component 2:
Component 3:	Component 3:
Component 4:	Component 4:

Summary Sheet: Areas of Desired Change and Action

1. Areas needing improvement or change (from student, staff, and community surveys)

    a.

    b.

    c.

    d.

2. Possible causes of safety concerns in these areas

    a.

    b.

    c.

    d.

3. Desired actions

    a.

    b.

    c.

    d.

Safe School Work Sheet 6

Developing Our Goal(s)

1. Based on the analysis of data and major areas of desired change, our priorities for action are as follows:

   a.

   b.

   c.

   d.

   e.

2. Our overall goal(s) for the _____-_____ school year is (are):

   a.

   b.

Action Plan for Component 1

Personal Characteristics of Students and Staff

The traits that students, teachers, administrators, and other personnel bring to the campus (ethnic/cultural diversity, different experiences)

Our goal is:

A. Areas of pride and desired change:

B. Objective 1:

   1. Related activities:

   2. Resources needed:

   3. Person(s) responsible for implementation:

   4. Timeline for implementation:

C. Objective 2:

   1. Related activities:

   2. Resources needed:

   3. Person(s) responsible for implementation:

   4. Timeline for implementation:

(Continue the process with items 1 through 4 for each objective.)

D. Budget:

E. Evaluation criteria and timeline:

Action Plan for Component 2

School's Physical Environment
The physical conditions in which education takes place (location, buildings, classrooms)

Our goal is:

A. Areas of pride and desired change:

B. Objective 1:

   1. Related activities:

   2. Resources needed:

   3. Person(s) responsible for implementation:

   4. Timeline for implementation:

C. Objective 2:

   1. Related activities:

   2. Resources needed:

   3. Person(s) responsible for implementation:

   4. Timeline for implementation:

   (Continue the process with items 1 through 4 for each objective.)

D. Budget:

E. Evaluation criteria and timeline:

Action Plan for Component 3

School's Social Environment

The organizational and interpersonal processes that occur in and around the school (structure, procedures, and organization)

Our goal is:

A. Areas of pride and desired change:

B. Objective 1:

    1. Related activities:

    2. Resources needed:

    3. Person(s) responsible for implementation:

    4. Timeline for implementation:

C. Objective 2:

    1. Related activities:

    2. Resources needed:

    3. Person(s) responsible for implementation:

    4. Timeline for implementation:

(Continue the process with items 1 through 4 for each objective.)

D. Budget:

E. Evaluation criteria and timeline:

Action Plan for Component 4

School's Culture
The general atmosphere or spirit of the school (norms, beliefs, and values)

Our goal is:

A. Areas of pride and desired change:

B. Objective 1:

    1. Related activities:

    2. Resources needed:

    3. Person(s) responsible for implementation:

    4. Timeline for implementation:

C. Objective 2:

    1. Related activities:

    2. Resources needed:

    3. Person(s) responsible for implementation:

    4. Timeline for implementation:

(Continue the process with items 1 through 4 for each objective.)

D. Budget:

E. Evaluation criteria and timeline:

Sample Action Plan for Component 1

Personal Characteristics of Students and Staff

The traits that students, teachers, administrators, and other personnel bring to the campus
(ethnic/cultural diversity, different experiences)

Our goal is: To reduce the emerging gang presence and influence on the _____ High School campus

A. *Areas of pride and desired change*

The Safe School Planning Committee recognizes and commends the students, staff, parents, and community businesses for the following conditions and programs at _____ High School that positively affect the physical and psychological well-being of all persons on campus:

- The outstanding, nationally recognized student assistance program
- The innovative and excellent student support services counseling program, which strives to provide individual counseling of the highest quality for every student
- The rich ethnic and cultural diversity among the student population, which allows for exposure to other cultures and an awareness and appreciation of those cultures by all concerned
- The ongoing programs (ESL, Sheltered English Strategies, strong bilingual programs) that assist students whose primary language orientation is not English

B. *Objective 1.* By the end of this school year, at least 10 percent of the gang members or students with the potential for gang involvement will participate in an at-risk support group program.

  1. Related activities:
      a. At least four community therapists will facilitate two small groups throughout the school year.
      b. XYZ community agency will facilitate at least one alternative activity per month.
      c. Counselor X and the chamber of commerce education committee will pair each student with an adult mentor.

  2. Resources needed:
      a. Community and staff persons who are willing to work with the small groups and are comfortable with becoming involved in the lives of young people who are involved in gangs
      b. Budgetary resources to cover small stipends for the leaders in this program
      c. A school-site policy mandating referral to such groups and the participation therein of students involved in gang-related incidents and allowing inclusion in such groups of students referred by parents or probation officers or those wishing to seek self-referral

3. Person(s) responsible for implementation: Safe School Planning Committee

4. Timeline for implementation: Program guidelines to be developed by December 1 and implemented no later than the second semester

C. *Objective 2.* Provide four parent support and education programs during the school year for at least 200 parents. Programs are to be designed especially for those parents whose high school children are already involved in or are moving in the direction of being involved in gang activity. Such groups would focus on gang education awareness and parenting techniques to restore positive parental control and would include small group interaction and support.

1. Related activities:

   a. The vice principal will identify 25 parents whose children are already involved in or are moving in the direction of being involved in gangs.
   b. The health education teacher and community agencies will schedule and plan four parent education programs.
   c. A community therapist will facilitate one parent support group per week.

2. Resources needed:

   a. Trained community or staff persons capable of and interested in leading such groups
   b. Budgetary resources to cover small stipends for participants' (leaders') time and involvement in such programs
   c. Budgetary resources to cover printed material for such programs
   d. Means of reaching community parents in need of such programs

3. Person(s) responsible for implementation: Safe School Planning Committee

4. Timeline for implementation: No later than the second semester

D. *Objective 3.* Develop an intensive in-service program designed to increase the awareness of every staff person at _____ High School to signs and symptoms of gang involvement and street gang culture and to teach staff persons methods for dealing with gang-related behavior. The program shall include specific, identifiable strategies for successfully combating the growing gang presence and culture within the school and require each participant to develop such strategies within the scope of his or her particular job responsibilities.

1. Related activities:

   a. The school resource officer will investigate gang prevention curricula and bring at least four samples back to the committee by November 1.
   b. The principal will schedule at least three staff trainings focusing on gang prevention techniques.

2. Resources needed:

   a. Development of in-service content and format
   b. Qualified presenters (security, law enforcement partnership)
   c. Method of assigning participants so that all staff have the opportunity to participate

3. Person(s) responsible for implementation:

   Shelly Ball, School-site Principal
   Miguel Francisco, Chief of District Security

4. Timeline for implementation: Entire staff to complete in-service training by May

E. *Budget*

1. Establishment of gang-intervention groups (stipends for leaders, materials, alternative activities, and so forth) $2,000

2. Establishment of parent support groups for parents of gang-involved children (stipends for teachers, materials) 1,200

3. Staff in-service program materials 100

4. Increased cultural awareness activities 1,000

F. *Evaluation criteria and timeline*

   Collect the following data at the end of the school year:

1. The number of youths participating in groups

   Compile statistics on the number of youths suspected of gang-related activity one year from the start of the program compared with the number at the beginning of the program.

2. The number of parents participating in groups

   Conduct parent surveys at the end of year to gauge the effectiveness of the program in improving family interactions.

3. Staff surveys on the effectiveness of the program

Safe School Work Sheet 8

Overall Timeline

Action Plan Objectives and Activities	Date to Be Completed												Person(s) Responsible
	J	A	S	O	N	D	J	F	M	A	M	J	
Action Plan Objective #___: **Activities:**													
Action Plan Objective #___: **Activities:**													
Action Plan Objective #___: **Activities:**													

Safe School Work Sheet 9

Evaluating Specific Objectives

Our Goal Is:

_____

_____

_____

Objective 1: _____

_____

Evaluation criteria and timeline:_____

Achievement level: _____

Comments: _____

Objective 2: _____

_____

Evaluation criteria and timeline:_____

Achievement level: _____

Comments: _____

Objective 3: _____

_____

Evaluation criteria and timeline:_____

Achievement level: _____

Comments: _____

Safe School Work Sheet 10

Evaluating and Assessing Our Progress

1. Monitor the implementation of the plan.

2. Determine whether the goals are being achieved.

3. Reassess the safe school vision, committee membership, and priorities.

Comments:

_____

_____

_____

_____

_____

Personal Characteristics of Students and Staff

Directions: This is a general questionnaire to be completed by students and staff. It includes questions about conditions that might affect the safety climate of the school. To answer, place an "X" on one of the five lines following each factor. There are no right or wrong answers. Do **not** put your name on this form.

When you have completed this form, please return it to _____ by _____.

Do any of the following factors **affect the safety of your school?**

Students' economic background

This is a concern. ____ ____ ____ ____ ____ This is not a concern.
              1   2   3   4   5

Home issues

This is a concern. ____ ____ ____ ____ ____ This is not a concern.
              1   2   3   4   5

Student/staff health

This is a concern. ____ ____ ____ ____ ____ This is not a concern.
              1   2   3   4   5

Campus ethnic/racial composition

This is a concern. ____ ____ ____ ____ ____ This is not a concern.
              1   2   3   4   5

Staff experience

This is a concern. ____ ____ ____ ____ ____ This is not a concern.
              1   2   3   4   5

Bullying

This is a concern. ____ ____ ____ ____ ____ This is not a concern.
              1   2   3   4   5

Alcohol and other drug use

This is a concern. ____ ____ ____ ____ ____ This is not a concern.
              1   2   3   4   5

Gang activity

This is a concern. ____ ____ ____ ____ ____ This is not a concern.
              1   2   3   4   5

Suicide

This is a concern. ____ ____ ____ ____ ____ This is not a concern.
              1   2   3   4   5

Please state on the reverse side any other conditions that you think influence the general safety of this school.

The School's Physical Environment: A Physical Security Survey

Directions: This list was developed to guide the safe school committee's evaluation of the essential elements of the school's physical safety. *True* responses indicate safe school conditions. Evaluate your school with respect to each question by placing an *X* on the line labeled *True* or *False*. After completing this assessment, record particular physical safety issues on "Safe School Work Sheet 4: Data Summary."

School location

True   *False*

_____   _____   1.   Our school is visible from neighboring homes, businesses, and roadways.

_____   _____   2.   There are no commercial activities in the immediate vicinity of the school that would adversely affect the school environment.

_____   _____   3.   There are no businesses near the school that draw students from the campus or attract people who pose a threat to the students.

School grounds

_____   _____   4.   All entries to our campus are properly secured.

_____   _____   5.   Security and local police have vehicle access to the campus at all times.

_____   _____   6.   Gates and door locks are accessible to police and fire personnel during emergencies.

_____   _____   7.   Local police are familiar enough with the campus to assist staff during emergencies or with visitor control.

_____   _____   8.   Field areas are fenced to prevent access by unauthorized vehicles and persons.

_____   _____   9.   School building areas are fenced separately from play areas to prevent intrusion during nonschool hours.

_____   _____   10.   The entry of visitors and outsiders onto the campus is controlled.

_____   _____   11.   There are signs at all entry points listing regulations and trespass laws.

_____   _____   12.   Visitors' entrances are clearly designated.

_____   _____   13.   The school grounds are clean.

_____   _____   14.   The grounds are free of rocks and gravel or other debris that might be used to vandalize the school property.

_____   _____   15.   The school-site design facilitates supervision (i.e., all gathering areas are clearly visible).

True	False	
_____	_____	16. Parking areas are visible from occupied building areas.
_____	_____	17. Bicycles are stored in secured areas during school hours.
_____	_____	18. Curbs around drives or parking areas are square in style to discourage the access of unauthorized vehicles to the grounds or building areas.
_____	_____	19. All necessary barriers exist to prevent the access of unauthorized vehicles to the campus.
_____	_____	20. There is a clear policy on maximum lighting overnight or no lighting (lights out) on the campus.
_____	_____	21. Exterior lighting is properly directed and bright enough to illuminate the necessary areas.
_____	_____	22. Lights are equipped with break-resistant lenses.
_____	_____	23. Damage caused by graffiti, broken glass, and other acts of vandalism is immediately repaired (before school opens).

School buildings/classrooms

_____	_____	24. The building design facilitates supervision (i.e., all areas in and around buildings are easily visible to staff and supervisors).
_____	_____	25. The school consults regularly with a locksmith and the police regarding building security.
_____	_____	26. All door and window locks have been checked recently to see whether they comply with updated crime prevention strategies.
_____	_____	27. There is a key-control system.
_____	_____	28. Locks on all exterior doors to high-risk areas are dead bolts.
_____	_____	29. All exterior doors have solid cores.
_____	_____	30. No exterior doors can be opened by breaking out nearby glass and reaching in.
_____	_____	31. All exterior doors open inwards.
_____	_____	32. Ground-floor windows have extra security precautions.
_____	_____	33. Break-resistant glass is used, especially in high-risk areas.
_____	_____	34. Large windows have been replaced with smaller windows.
_____	_____	35. There are no sliding or casement windows that can be easily forced open on campus buildings.
_____	_____	36. Graffiti-resistant paint is used on buildings.
_____	_____	37. Signs use painted lettering or engraved lettering only.
_____	_____	38. Roofs are accessible only by ladder.

True   *False*

_____   _____   39. Roofs are fire retardant.

_____   _____   40. Buildings and classrooms have adequate communication systems (telephones, intercoms, and so forth).

Internal security: school alarms

_____   _____   41. Buildings are fitted with fire alarms and automatic fire-control sprinklers.

_____   _____   42. Facilities have been inspected recently by fire prevention personnel to detect possible code violations or to make fire prevention suggestions.

_____   _____   43. A burglar-alarm system is installed and integrated throughout the campus.

_____   _____   44. The alarm system(s) is easily used by the staff.

_____   _____   45. The capabilities and limitations of the alarm system are understood by all.

_____   _____   46. The alarm system(s) is regularly maintained and tested.

_____   _____   47. Police, security, and fire departments are alerted by the alarm system(s).

Internal security: school property

_____   _____   48. There is an up-to-date inventory (either written or computerized) of equipment and valuable property.

_____   _____   49. Property is inventoried on videotape for easy identification.

_____   _____   50. Equipment is engraved with the school name and school property identification number.

_____   _____   51. Valuables and equipment are properly secured.

_____   _____   52. School files and records are kept in a fire-proof safe or storage area.

Thank you for your help.

Safe School Questionnaire 3

Our School's Safety

(Questionnaire for Adults)

Directions: As a part of the safe school committee's efforts to develop a safe school plan, we are seeking your opinion about how you feel about the school. Indicate your opinions by circling one number to the right of each item. Do **not** put your name on this form.

	Strongly Disagree	Disagree	Neutral	Agree	Strongly Agree
1. There are few locations near campus that encourage crime.	1	2	3	4	5
2. The effects of vandalism on campus are quickly repaired.	1	2	3	4	5
3. The school buildings are free of hazards that might cause accidental injury.	1	2	3	4	5
4. Staff use standard definitions and procedures to identify school crime.	1	2	3	4	5
5. The principal seeks comments from students and staff before making important decisions.	1	2	3	4	5
6. The school has adequate resources to help students in emergency situations.	1	2	3	4	5
7. Every effort is made to use all class time for instructional activities and lessons.	1	2	3	4	5
8. Many parents are actively involved in school matters and decision making.	1	2	3	4	5
9. Everyone shares a feeling of wanting the school to change and grow in positive ways.	1	2	3	4	5
10. Students and staff have a sincere concern about each other.	1	2	3	4	5
11. The rules and expectations are clear and well known to everyone at school.	1	2	3	4	5

	Strongly Disagree	Disagree	Neutral	Agree	Strongly Agree
12. The rules and regulations are written and posted throughout the school (handbook distributed).	1	2	3	4	5
13. The people at this school value learning and want to learn new skills.	1	2	3	4	5
14. Instructional time is used productively by students and teachers.	1	2	3	4	5
15. The consequences of violating school rules are fair and known to all and are applied consistently.	1	2	3	4	5
16. The rewards used at the school are appropriate and meaningful.	1	2	3	4	5
17. Positive behavior is acknowledged frequently. Students and staff feel appreciated.	1	2	3	4	5
18. The school is well protected from potential crime or vandalism.	1	2	3	4	5
19. The school is well maintained and a pleasant place in which to spend time.	1	2	3	4	5
20. The classrooms are well maintained and inviting places in which to learn.	1	2	3	4	5
21. Law enforcement personnel are involved in campus activities in nonenforcement roles.	1	2	3	4	5
22. The procedures used to make decisions at school are well known to students and staff.	1	2	3	4	5
23. There are clear procedures to deal with emergencies.	1	2	3	4	5
24. Every attempt is made to place students in heterogeneous classes, except for mathematics and reading.	1	2	3	4	5
25. Many students participate in school events.	1	2	3	4	5
26. In this school almost everyone can be trusted, and students and staff feel physically and psychologically safe.	1	2	3	4	5

		Strongly Disagree	Disagree	Neutral	Agree	Strongly Agree
27.	Students and staff feel it is their responsibility to improve this school.	1	2	3	4	5
28.	School rules and expectations are realistic, practical, fair, and relevant to the students and staff.	1	2	3	4	5
29.	There is a tone of high moral standards, positive messages, and high expectations of everyone at this school.	1	2	3	4	5
30.	Everyone at this school can be successful.	1	2	3	4	5
31.	Disciplinary practices focus on the causes of problems and provide problem-solving procedures, rather than just punitive reactions.	1	2	3	4	5
32.	At this school it is everyone's responsibility to see that school rules are followed.	1	2	3	4	5
33.	People at this school receive public recognition for their good efforts.	1	2	3	4	5
34.	Few conditions on campus could cause accidental injury.	1	2	3	4	5
35.	The school buildings are in good condition.	1	2	3	4	5
36.	The classrooms have adequate space for the student-teacher ratio.	1	2	3	4	5
37.	The community uses the school during nonschool hours.	1	2	3	4	5
38.	Students and staff are allowed to make decisions and choices whenever appropriate.	1	2	3	4	5
39.	The principal provides leadership in curriculum development.	1	2	3	4	5
40.	Every effort is made to encourage cooperation among students in the classroom.	1	2	3	4	5

	Strongly Disagree	Disagree	Neutral	Agree	Strongly Agree
41. There is clear coordination between the school and other public agencies, such as the police, county juvenile probation officers, and county mental health personnel.	1	2	3	4	5
42. Students, staff, and parents feel personally responsible for what happens at school.	1	2	3	4	5
43. Everyone's racial and ethnic heritage is respected at this school.	1	2	3	4	5
44. The entire school community participates in developing behavioral expectations.	1	2	3	4	5
45. The people at this school believe it is important to be productive.	1	2	3	4	5
46. Academic expectations are clear and positive for all students.	1	2	3	4	5
47. There are clear procedures for reporting all criminal behaviors to law enforcement agencies.	1	2	3	4	5
48. The principal and staff show respect, consideration, and sensitivity to students and parents.	1	2	3	4	5
49. The principal is highly visible on campus and is available to all members of the school community.	1	2	3	4	5
50. Equipment is inventoried and engraved for easy identification.	1	2	3	4	5
51. Classrooms are orderly and focused on instruction.	1	2	3	4	5
52. Parents and volunteers are recruited as monitors.	1	2	3	4	5
53. Parents, teachers, and community members are encouraged to participate in school activities.	1	2	3	4	5
54. Students and staff work together, with a minimum of favoritism shown.	1	2	3	4	5

Please make any comments you may have about our school's safety in the space below.

Thank you for your help.

Safe School Questionnaire 4

Our School's Safety

(Questionnaire for Students)

Grade: _____

Directions: The safe school committee needs to determine how safe you feel on campus. We also want to hear about the things at school that you feel are unsafe and how they can be made safer. Do **not** put your name on this form, but do note your grade level.

Please show your opinions by circling one number for each statement that best shows your feelings about this school.

		Strongly Disagree	Disagree	Neutral	Agree	Strongly Agree
1.	There are no places near this school that scare me.	1	2	3	4	5
2.	They take good care of the school yard.	1	2	3	4	5
3.	There is a lot of space in the classrooms at this school.	1	2	3	4	5
4.	There are law enforcement officers who work here on campus.	1	2	3	4	5
5.	When students at this school have an emergency, someone is there to help.	1	2	3	4	5
6.	Teachers at this school let me do projects and assignments with other students in the class.	1	2	3	4	5
7.	I really want this school to be "the best."	1	2	3	4	5
8.	I feel that I belong in this school.	1	2	3	4	5
9.	I work very hard in all my classes.	1	2	3	4	5
10.	When students break rules, they all receive the same treatment.	1	2	3	4	5
11.	I feel safe at this school.	1	2	3	4	5
12.	The buildings at this school look in good condition.	1	2	3	4	5

		Strongly Disagree	Disagree	Neutral	Agree	Strongly Agree
13.	Strangers do not come and go from school easily.	1	2	3	4	5
14.	The principal asks students about their ideas at this school.	1	2	3	4	5
15.	We do not waste time in our classes at this school.	1	2	3	4	5
16.	You can trust people at this school.	1	2	3	4	5
17.	Everyone is expected to be his or her best at this school.	1	2	3	4	5
18.	Students at this school really want to learn.	1	2	3	4	5
19.	Teachers go out of their way to let me know I am doing a good job.	1	2	3	4	5
20.	Only a few students get hurt in accidents at this school.	1	2	3	4	5
21.	Very few accidents happen inside the buildings at this school.	1	2	3	4	5
22.	Students are given many choices at this school.	1	2	3	4	5
23.	My parents are involved at this school.	1	2	3	4	5
24.	Blacks, Hispanics, Asians, Whites, and all other students are respected at this school.	1	2	3	4	5
25.	The school rules are listed in the classrooms and distributed around the school, and students know what the rules are.	1	2	3	4	5
26.	I can be a success in school.	1	2	3	4	5
27.	It pays to follow the rules and do well at this school.	1	2	3	4	5
28.	Writing on walls is cleaned or painted over quickly at this school.	1	2	3	4	5
29.	The classrooms at this school look very nice.	1	2	3	4	5

		Strongly Disagree	Disagree	Neutral	Agree	Strongly Agree
30.	In some classes I am with students of different abilities and talents.	1	2	3	4	5
31.	Most students get involved in school activities.	1	2	3	4	5
32.	People care for each other at this school.	1	2	3	4	5
33.	The rules at this school are fair.	1	2	3	4	5
34.	Teachers at this school look out for troublemakers.	1	2	3	4	5
35.	We learn things about ourselves and about life and other things in addition to regular subjects.	1	2	3	4	5
36.	Parents often serve as hall and playground monitors at this school.	1	2	3	4	5

37. Which of these things happened to you in *the past month:*

a.	I was pushed around by someone who was just being mean.	NO	YES
b.	I was in a fistfight with another student.	NO	YES
c.	I was robbed or had something stolen from me.	NO	YES
d.	I saw a student with a knife.	NO	YES
e.	I saw a student with a gun.	NO	YES
f.	I saw students use drugs or alcohol on campus.	NO	YES
g.	I saw students steal from the library, a classroom, or the cafeteria.	NO	YES
h.	I saw someone destroy or make marks on school equipment or buildings (walls).	NO	YES
i.	I was afraid of being beaten up on the way to or from school.	NO	YES
j.	I was afraid of gang activity at school.	NO	YES
k.	I was threatened by someone with a knife or gun.	NO	YES
l.	I was called names or put down by other students.	NO	YES
m.	I felt rejected by other students.	NO	YES
n.	I saw students smoking or chewing tobacco on campus.	NO	YES
o.	I know students who came to school high on drugs or alcohol.	NO	YES

38.   You probably have other ideas about how to make our school safer. Please write your ideas in the space below.

Thank you for your help.

Safe School Tally Sheet 1

Our School's Safety

(Tally Sheet for Adults)

Directions:

1. Record the answers (1 through 5) for each item from "Safe School Questionnaire 3: Our School's Safety." For example, if three people responded with "1" for *Strongly Disagree* and four people chose "3" for *Neutral* on the same question, you would record (3×1) + (4×3), or 15, next to that question number on this tally sheet.

2. Add all items in each element and record the total on the line marked *Sum.*

3. Divide the sum by the number of items in each element.

4. Divide your answer by the number of respondents.

5. Record the average score in the space provided. This number relates to the response categories (1=Strongly Disagree through 5= Strongly Agree).

6. By averaging all the scores from each of the responses (by category), you will get a picture of the opinion of the whole school.

The School's Physical Environment

School location	1. _____	Average score = _____
School grounds	2. _____	Sum _____
	18. _____	Divide by 4 _____
	19. _____	Divide by number of respondents _____
	34. _____	Average score = _____
School buildings	3. _____	Sum _____
	35. _____	Divide by 2 _____
		Divide by number of respondents _____
		Average score = _____
School classrooms	20. _____	Sum _____
	36. _____	Divide by 2 _____
		Divide by number of respondents _____
		Average score = _____

Internal security   4. ____   Sum ____

                        37. ____   Divide by 4 ____

                        41. ____   Divide by number of respondents ____

                        50. ____   Average score = ____

The School's Social Environment

Leadership   5. ____   Sum ____

                        39. ____   Divide by 4 ____

                        48. ____   Divide by number of respondents ____

                        49. ____   Average score = ____

School-site management   6. ____   Sum ____

                        22. ____   Divide by 4 ____

                        23. ____   Divide by number of respondents ____

                        38. ____   Average score = ____

Classroom organization
and structure   7. ____   Sum ____

                        24. ____   Divide by 4 ____

                        40. ____   Divide by number of respondents ____

                        51. ____   Average score = ____

Discipline and
consequences   15. ____   Sum ____

                        31. ____   Divide by 4 ____

                        32. ____   Divide by number of respondents ____

                        47. ____   Average score = ____

Participation and
involvement   8. ____   Sum ____

                        21. ____   Divide by 7 ____

                        25. ____   Divide by number of respondents ____

                        27. ____   Average score = ____

                        42. ____

                        52. ____

                        53. ____

The School's Culture

Affiliation and bonding		
9. ____	Sum ____
10. ____	Divide by 5 ____
26. ____	Divide by number of respondents ____
43 ____	Average score = ____
54. ____	

Behavioral expectations		
11. ____	Sum ____
12. ____	Divide by 5 ____
28. ____	Divide by number of respondents ____
29. ____	Average score = ____
44. ____	

Academic expectations		
13. ____	Sum ____
14. ____	Divide by 5 ____
30. ____	Divide by number of respondents ____
45. ____	Average score = ____
46. ____	

Support and recognition		
16. ____	Sum ____
17. ____	Divide by 3 ____
33. ____	Divide by number of respondents ____
	Average score = ____

Our School's Safety

(Tally Sheet for Students)

Directions:

1. Record the answers (1 through 5) for each item from "Safe School Questionnaire 4." For example, if three people responded with "1" for *Strongly Disagree* and four people chose "3" for *Neutral* on the same question, you would record (3×1) + (4×3), or 15, next to that question number on this tally sheet.

2. Add all items in each element and record the total on the line marked *Sum.*

3. Divide the sum by the number of items in each element.

4. Divide your answer by the number of respondents.

5. Record the average score in the space provided. This number relates to the response categories (1=Strongly Disagree through 5= Strongly Agree).

6. By averaging all the scores from each of the responses (by category), you will get a picture of the opinion of the whole school.

The School's Physical Environment

School location   1. ____   Score = _____

School grounds   2. ____   Sum _____
                        11. ____   Divide by 4 _____
                        20. ____   Divide by number of respondents _____
                        28. ____   Average score = _____

School buildings   12. ____   Sum _____
                        21. ____   Divide by 2 _____
                                          Divide by number of respondents _____
                                          Average score = _____

School classrooms   3. ____   Sum ____
                        29. ____   Divide by 2 _____
                                          Divide by number of respondents _____
                                          Average score = _____

Internal security   13. ____   Sum ____
                              36. ____   Divide by 2 ____
                                           Divide by number of respondents ____
                                           Average score = ____

The School's Social Environment

Leadership   14. ____   Average score = ____

School-site management   5. ____   Sum ____
                              22. ____   Divide by 2 ____
                                           Divide by number of respondents ____
                                           Average score = ____

Classroom organization and structure   6. ____   Sum ____
                              15. ____   Divide by 4 ____
                              30. ____   Divide by number of respondents ____
                              35. ____   Average score = ____

Discipline and consequences   10. ____   Sum ____
                              27. ____   Divide by 3 ____
                              34. ____   Divide by number of respondents ____
                                           Average score = ____

Participation an involvement   4. ____   Sum ____
                              7. ____   Divide by 4 ____
                              23. ____   Divide by number of respondents ____
                              31. ____   Average score = ____

The School's Culture

Affiliation and bonding   8. ____   Sum ____
                              16. ____   Divide by 4 ____
                              24. ____   Divide by number of respondents ____
                              32. ____   Average score = ____

Behavioral expectations   17. ____   Sum _____

                                    25. ____   Divide by 3 _____

                                    33. ____   Divide by number of respondents _____

                                                              Average score = _____

Academic expectations   9. ____   Sum _____

                                    18. ____   Divide by 3 _____

                                    26. ____   Divide by number of respondents _____

                                                              Average score = _____

Support and recognition   19. ____   Average score = _____

37. Record the number of reported incidents per category:

     a. ____ Bullying/assault

     b. ____ Fighting

     c. ____ Theft (personal)

     d. ____ Saw knife

     e. ____ Saw gun

     f. ____ Saw drugs/alcohol

     g. ____ Theft (school)

     h. ____ Vandalism

     i. ____ Fear going to and from school

     j. ____ Fear gangs

     k. ____ Threatened with weapon

     l. ____ Verbal attack

     m. ____ Social isolation

     n. ____ Tobacco use

     o. ____ Saw intoxicated students

Safe School Tally Sheet 3

Observation List

Responses by students and staff to questionnaires provide valuable information about the general perceptions each group has about the school. The behaviors of students and staff also provide information about each group's perceptions of school safety. For example, the students' beliefs about teacher accessibility can be assessed by counting the number of student-initiated meetings with teachers. The following list of behaviors or conditions may be assessed through an informal observational method. The school planning committee can select or identify the particular behaviors or conditions it wants to evaluate.

The School's Physical Environment

1. Count the number of open classroom doors.

2. How often and when is the office door open?

3. What smell does the campus have (pleasant or unpleasant)?

4. Are student voices heard throughout the day? Are they a source of pleasure or irritation?

5. How often can music be heard on campus?

6. How many "cozy corners" can be found in classrooms and elsewhere on campus?

7. Are student collections and hobbies evident on campus?

8. Is student work displayed in public places?

9. How many classrooms have bolted-down desks?

10. How many persons in the school have master keys?

11. How many times during the day do bells ring?

12. How many graffiti are evident? How quickly do graffiti return after being removed?

13. Does the parking lot have spaces reserved for administrators?

14. How many windows have been broken this year?

15. How many toilets have been deliberately plugged this school year?

16. How many bulletin boards or display cases are empty?

17. How many display cases have not been redecorated in years?

18. How many newly planted flowers are on campus?

19. How long has it been since the school was painted?

20. How many parents and visitors comment about the appearance of the school campus?

21. How many student accidents and injuries have there been in the past year?

22. How many muddy, bare spots are on campus?

23. How often is broken glass found on campus?

24. What is the height of the fence surrounding the school?

The School's Social Environment

1. How often do students make significant choices (in classes and in helping to run the school)?

2. How often do students seek help from school or community resource personnel?

3. How often are students involved in planning learning activities?

4. How often are students involved in planning social events?

5. How often are students involved in setting up bulletin boards or displays?

6. How often do students ask questions in class? Of their counselors? Of the principal?

7. What percentage of students are seen smiling and laughing during the school day?

8. What percentage of students play games or interact pleasantly during breaks?

9. What percentage of students carry nonrequired reading material?

10. What percentage of students are involved in extracurricular activities?

11. How many students attend optional school events?

12. How many teachers provide a variety of learning choices for students?

13. How often are teachers and staff seen listening to students?

14. What is the ratio of positive to negative comments made about students in the teachers' lounge?

15. How often do teachers and staff volunteer their own time for school activities?

16. How often do teachers and staff voluntarily stay after school to help students?

17. How many parents volunteer their help with school projects and activities?

18. How many in-service activities does the administration support each year?

19. How many educational alternatives are available?

20. How many changes in administration have occurred during the past five years?

21. What percentage of teachers have been at the school for more than five years?

22. How many threatening notes or telephone calls has the school received?

23. How many staff meeting agenda items do not deal with instruction?

24. How many staff meeting agenda items are proposed by teachers and other staff?

25. What is the talking-listening ratio of administrators and teachers at staff meetings?

26. How many items at staff meetings are generated by students?

27. How many public-address announcements are made each day?

28. How many school activities are parents invited to attend?

29. What percentage of parents come to school activities when invited?

30. How many community volunteers work in the school?

31. How many staff and students recognize the school district superintendent?

32. How often do administrators visit classrooms and attend school activities?

The School's Culture

1. How many students go to the library by choice, not just for assignments?

2. What percentage of students are assigned homework each school night?

3. What percentage of students complete their daily class and homework assignments?

4. What percentage of students drop out each year?

5. What percentage of students skip class each day?

6. How many students have been arrested this year?

7. How many students have run away from home this year?

8. How many students have attempted suicide this school year?

9. How many students know the principal's name, age, likes, dislikes, and so forth?

10. How many students do not return to class after a fire drill?

11. How many students left school because of pregnancy this year?

12. How many students come to class "stoned" or under the influence of drugs or alcohol?

13. What percentage of the student body are habitual smokers?

14. How often are students encouraged to do their best?

15. How often are students told how they are doing in their classes?

16. How many students have been suspended or expelled this year?

17. How many false fire alarms have been set this year?

18. How many bomb threats have been received by telephone?

19. What percentage of the administrator's time is devoted to discipline?

20. What is the ratio of hall monitors to students?

21. How many faculty cars have been damaged in the school parking lot this past year?

22. How many times have the police been called to campus during the past year?

23. How many rules in the student handbook use the word "don't"?

24. How many staff members voluntarily eat with the students?

Appendix H

Interagency Information Exchange Forms

The safe school committee will need to modify the following sample forms for its own jurisdiction to obtain access to records it needs for collecting all available school safety data. The forms provide a beginning for interagency work. Because these are samples, it would be advisable to check them with your county council after the participating agencies agree to co-operate.

- "Court Order Allowing Interagency Information Exchange" is very broad and covers multiple access to the records of many agencies.

- "Court Order Authorizing School–Probation Information Exchange" deals only with the records of the two entities named.

- "Superior Court . . . Miscellaneous Order" sets a framework for the exchange of information.

- "Interagency Case Information Request" can be used to manage the flow of records among all participating agencies.

- "Confidential Information Requested" is a form for requesting information from the appropriate agency.

- "Consent to Release Confidential Information" is a form for obtaining the signed consent of the minor and parent to receipt and exchange of records.

Sample

COURT ORDER
ALLOWING INTERAGENCY INFORMATION EXCHANGE

State of _____, Superior Court
County of _____, Juvenile Court

ORDER OF THE JUVENILE COURT AUTHORIZING RELEASE AND EXCHANGE OF INFORMATION AMONG SCHOOL DISTRICTS, LAW ENFORCEMENT AGENCIES, PROSECUTORS, COUNTY COUNSELS, CHILD PROTECTIVE SERVICES, AND PROBATION DEPARTMENTS OF _____ COUNTY.

Pursuant to the authority vested in the court by Sections 827 and 828 of the *Welfare and Institutions Code* and Section 49077 of the *Education Code*, IT IS HEREBY ORDERED that juvenile court records and any other information that may be in the possession of school districts, law enforcement agencies, prosecutors, county counsels, child protective service agencies, and probation departments regarding minors may be released, for governmental purposes only, to the following persons who have a legitimate and official interest in the information:

1. The minor
2. The minor's attorney
3. The minor's parents or guardians
4. Foster parents
5. All district attorneys' offices
6. All law enforcement agencies
7. All county attorneys
8. All school districts
9. All probation departments
10. All public welfare agencies
11. All youth detention facilities
12. All corrections departments
13. Authorized court personnel
14. All courts
15. Treatment or placement programs that require information for placement, treatment, or rehabilitation of minors
16. All multidisciplinary teams for abuse, neglect, or delinquency
17. All juvenile justice citizens advisory boards
18. All state central information registries
19. All coroners
20. All victims may receive information from law enforcement agencies, probation departments, or the prosecutor to enable them to pursue civil remedies. These same agencies may release information to identifiable potential victims that a minor constitutes a threat to their person or property. They may release the name, description, and whereabouts of the minor and the nature of the threat toward the potential victim.

All information received by the authorized recipients listed above may be further disseminated only to other authorized recipients without further order of this court.

_____   _____
Date   Presiding Judge, Juvenile Court

Sample

COURT ORDER
AUTHORIZING SCHOOL–PROBATION
INFORMATION EXCHANGE

State of _____, Superior Court

County of _____, Juvenile Court

ORDER OF THE JUVENILE COURT AUTHORIZING RELEASE AND EXCHANGE OF INFORMATION BETWEEN SCHOOL DISTRICTS AND PROBATION OFFICIALS

Pursuant to the authority vested in the Court by Sections 827 and 828 of the *Welfare and Institutions Code* and Section 49077 of the *Education Code*, IT IS HEREBY ORDERED that the Probation Department of _____ County and all school districts in _____ County shall release information to each other regarding all minors and students under their supervision. Information that may be helpful in providing juvenile court educational placements and in increasing school safety and other legitimate official concerns of both agencies shall be shared by both agencies. Such information shall include, but is not limited to, academic, attendance, and disciplinary records, arrest and dispositional data, names of minors on probation and their assigned probation officers, and names of minors attending individual schools and their assigned teacher, counselor, or other appropriate adult contact at the school site.

_____

Date

_____

Presiding Judge, Juvenile Court

Sample

SUPERIOR COURT OF THE STATE OF CALIFORNIA
IN AND FOR THE COUNTY OF _____
SITTING AS THE JUVENILE COURT
MISCELLANEOUS ORDER

WHEREAS, pursuant to Sections 827 and 828 of the California *Welfare and Institutions Code* and Section 49077 of the *Education Code*, the Court may authorize the disclosure of juvenile offender information and juvenile pupil information, respectively; and

WHEREAS, Article 1, Section 28(c) of the California Constitution likewise establishes the right of students and staff in kindergarten through grade twelve to "campuses which are safe, secure, and peaceful"; and

WHEREAS, youth gangs clearly imperil the safety of both students and campuses; and

WHEREAS, the Court has been informed that concerns about "confidentiality" often have hampered or prevented communication among educators, law enforcement officials, district attorney, and probation personnel; and

WHEREAS, the lack of communication among the various professionals dealing with the same child impedes the solving and prosecution of crimes, as well as the evaluation and placement of juveniles who have committed crimes, and thus deprives educators of information needed to ensure safer schools;

THEREFORE, IT IS ORDERED, that all school districts in _____ County, all police departments in _____ County, and _____ County District Attorney may release information to each other regarding any minor when any person employed by such department, office, or school district indicates that there is a reasonable belief that this minor is a gang member or at significant risk of becoming a gang member.

Dated this _____ day of _____, 19__.   _____

Presiding Judge, Juvenile Court

*Sample—to be printed on agency letterhead
or with combined names/logos of all participating agencies*

INTERAGENCY CASE INFORMATION REQUEST

Information requested by:

Name _____   Title _____

Mail to _____   Telephone _____

Needed by (date) _____

Supervisor's name _____   Telephone _____

Minor/student's name _____

Minor/student's address _____

Telephone _____   Birth date _____

School _____   Grade _____

Parent/guardian's name _____

Parent/guardian's address, if different from that of minor or student _____

_____

Telephone _____

Sample

CONFIDENTIAL INFORMATION REQUESTED

Check the requested information from the appropriate agency.

SCHOOLS

[ ] Attendance
[ ] Discipline
[ ] Academic achievement
[ ] Current progress
[ ] Special program placement
[ ] *Please call me*

PROBATION

[ ] Terms and conditions
[ ] Current progress
[ ] Arrest/disposition
[ ] *Please call me*

DISTRICT ATTORNEY

[ ] Case conferences
[ ] Progress of case
[ ] Court rulings
[ ] Victim/witness information
[ ] *Please call me*

LAW ENFORCEMENT

[ ] Arrest history
[ ] Diversions
[ ] Field interviews
[ ] Family arrest history
[ ] Gang involvement
[ ] *Please call me*

CHILD PROTECTIVE SERVICES

[ ] Abuse/neglect data
[ ] Current progress
[ ] Service plans
[ ] *Please call me*

INTERAGENCY TEAM

[ ] Petitions filed
[ ] Profiles/reports
[ ] Service plans
[ ] Current progress
[ ] *Please call me*

Sample—to be printed on agency letterhead
or with combined names/logos of all participating agencies

CONSENT TO RELEASE CONFIDENTIAL INFORMATION

I (child's parent or guardian), _____, hereby give the (agency's name)

_____ my consent to obtain confidential medical, psychological, drug and

alcohol treatment, mental health, other treatment, and educational information from and exchange

such confidential information with my child's physician, psychologist or counselor, social worker,

probation officer, and/or school officials. I understand that this information will be used by the juve-

nile court and the (agency's name) _____ to provide necessary services

and treatment as long as my child is under the jurisdiction of the juvenile court or I am or my child is

under the supervision of (agency's name) _____.

* * * * *

Minor's date of birth _____

Minor's current school or last school, if not presently enrolled _____

Minor's physician _____

Minor's counselor(s), psychologist, or psychiatrist _____

Minor's social worker _____

Minor's probation/parole officer _____

Parent's/guardian's signature _____ Date _____

Appendix I

Important School Safety Legal References

School Safety Issue	Code Reference
Access to juvenile court records	W&IC §§ 825–830, 504
Access to school premises (trespassers)	PC §§ 626, 627 et seq.; EC § 32211
Access to school record	20 USC 1238(g) (FERPA); EC §§ 49061–49077
Assault on school employee	PC § 241.6
BB guns and so forth	PC §§ 117(b), 417.2, 626.10, 417.4
Child abuse reporting	PC §§ 11164–11174.3
Confidential court reports to school district superintendent and employees re drugs and serious crimes by students	W&IC § 827(b)
Considerations requiring recommendation of expulsion or statement to governing board	EC § 48915(a), 48915(b)
Court terms of school attendance and required report of truancy to probation department	EC § 48267
Custodian of records	5 CCR 431
Detention after school	5 CCR 353
Detention during recess	EC § 44807.5
District liability	EC § 44808
District shall inform teachers of students who have violated Section 48900 (except[h]). Failure to do so is a misdemeanor.	EC § 49079
Dress codes	EC § 3518.3
Duplication or possession of keys	PC § 469
Electronic signaling devices	EC § 48901.5
Enrollment in community schools	EC § 48915.2, 48915.7

School Safety Issue *(Continued)*	Code Reference
Expulsion orders, and reasons for such, in student record; orders must be forwarded to any school in which student subsequently enrolls upon receipt of a request for such record	EC § 48918(j)
False bomb report	PC § 148.1
Freedom of expression	EC § 48907
Grounds for suspension	EC § 48900
Hearing required by the governing board for any student new to the district who has been expelled for the major crimes related to weapons and controlled substances, to determine continuing danger posed by student	EC § 48915.1(c)
Injurious objects, employee designated by governing board	EC §§ 49330–49333
Knowledge of rules of discipline	EC §§ 35291, 35291.5
Notice to district attorney of nonattendance	EC § 48263.5
Parent complaint	EC § 35160.5(c)
Parental liability	EC § 48904
Pending final determination of any dispute over a pending disciplinary decision, regardless of the degree of violence the pupil exhibits, a special education pupil cannot be suspended for more than 10 days.	*Honig v. Doe,* 484 U.S. 305 (1988); EC § 48915.5
Principal's responsibility for adequate certificated supervision	5 CCR 5552
Pupil liability	CC § 1714.1
Release of pupils to peace officer	EC § 48906
Required notice to parents re truancy	EC § 48260.5
Required reporting of assault by a pupil against a school employee (employee's supervisor also required to report such incidents)	EC § 44014
Right of public to place matters of school business on the board agenda	EC § 35145.5
Right to a safe school	California Constitution, Article I, Section 28(c)
Sales within 1,000 feet of school	H&SC § 11353.6
School district police/security departments	EC §§ 39670–39671; PC §§ 241.4, 626.9, 830.4, 1463.12; VC (CVC) § 165

School Safety Issue *(Continued)*	Code Reference
School safety model programs, conferences, and regional teams	EC §§ 32260 et seq.
Schools required to adopt site rules and procedures on discipline and solicit participation; notification requirements	EC §§ 35291 et seq.
Searches	EC § 49050
Shall notify law enforcement authorities within one day after suspension or expulsion of a student for an act that may violate EC 48900(c) or (d)	EC § 48902(b)
Shall report to law enforcement authorities any student involved with the possession or sale of narcotics or a controlled substance or in possession of a knife 2 1/2 inches long, a gun, a laser, or a stun gun	EC § 48902 et seq.
Shall report to law enforcement authorities any violation of PC § 245 (assault with deadly weapon) prior to suspension or expulsion of a student	EC § 48902(a)
Signed statement by staff re requirements to report child abuse	PC § 11166.5
Special education pupil cannot be expelled if the misbehavior for which expulsion is sought is a manifestation of the pupil's disability or the result of an inappropriate placement.	*Honig v. Doe*, 484 U.S. 305 (1988); EC § 48915.5
Standard school crime reporting form	PC §§ 628 et seq.
Students held to account/physical control	EC § 44807
Summary of state laws for schools (requires notice to parents)	PC § 626.1
Supervision, extracurricular activities of pupils	5 CCR 5531
Supervisor of attendance/apportionment, duties of	EC § 48240
Suspension as a last resort (consider alternatives, such as community service/school beautification)	EC § 48900.5
Suspension by a teacher (only for acts stated in EC § 48900)	EC § 48910
Suspension due-process report to governing board or district superintendent on each suspension; principal's designee defined	EC §§ 48911(e), 48911(i)

Appendix J

School/Law Enforcement Partnership Cadre Services

The Goal

The School/Law Enforcement Partnership cadre provides materials and assistance to schools and law enforcement agencies needing help in building community teams to address school safety issues. The goal of the cadre is to encourage school and law enforcement agencies to develop and implement interagency partnership programs, strategies, and activities that promote safe schools, improve school attendance, and encourage good citizenship. To achieve this goal, a cadre of professionals has been trained to provide free personal technical assistance and resource materials to schools, law enforcement organizations, and other youth-serving agencies.

Background

In 1983 the California Department of Justice and the Department of Education began the School/Law Enforcement Partnership. The California Legislature and the governor later endorsed the concept by enacting legislation (*Education Code* Section 32290) that provided funds for the School/Law Enforcement Partnership cadre.

Free Technical and Program Assistance

The cadre staff will personally contact you to link your agency with cadre members who can assist you in any of the following areas:

- Child abuse reporting/prevention
- Citizenship education
- Conflict management
- Drug and alcohol abuse prevention
- Formation of school/law enforcement partnerships

- Gang violence prevention
- Multicultural awareness/competence
- Parental education
- Peer counseling
- School Attendance Review Board (SARB)
- School climate
- School safety planning
- School security
- Subcults
- Suicide prevention
- Truancy/dropout reduction
- Vandalism reduction

Free Services

- Audiovisual and printed materials
- In-service workshops
- Program planning and development
- Staff development training
- Telephone consultations

How to Obtain Services

Assistance and materials for forming partnerships are available from the cadre at no cost. To obtain services, call or write to either of the following agencies:

School Safety and Violence Prevention Office
California Department of Education
P.O. Box 944272
Sacramento, CA 94244-2720
(916) 657-2989

Crime and Violence Prevention Center
Office of the Attorney General
California Department of Justice
P.O. Box 944255
Sacramento, CA 94244-2550
(916) 324-7863

Selected Resources

This list is arranged in three sections: publications, videotapes, and addresses of resource centers.

Publications

American Academy of Pediatrics, Committee on School Health Staff. "Violence in Schools: Current Status and Prevention," in *School Health: Policy and Practice.* Elk Grove Village, Ill.: American Academy of Pediatrics, 1993.

Biblio Alert! New Resources for Prevention of Injury and Violence. Arlington, Va.: Children's Safety Network, National Center for Education in Maternal and Child Health, 1993 (publications containing lists of current resources on topics related to child safety). Two of these issues are *Focus on Firearms* and *Alcohol and Injury.*

Boyer, Ernest L. "'Civic' Education for Responsible Citizens," *Educational Leadership,* Vol. 48 (November, 1990), 3, 4–7.

Child Abuse Prevention Handbook. Sacramento: Office of the California Attorney General, Crime and Violence Prevention Center, 1986.

Child Safety Curriculum Standards. Westlake Village, Calif.: National School Safety Center, 1992.

Criminal Victimization. Washington, D.C.: U.S. Department of Justice, Bureau of Justice Statistics, 1992.

DeJong, William. *Preventing Interpersonal Violence Among Youths: An Introduction to School, Community, and Mass Media Strategies.* Cambridge, Mass.: Harvard School of Public Health, 1994. Available from the National Criminal Justice Reference Service (see Resource Centers section).

Developing Personal and Social Responsibility. Westlake Village, Calif.: National School Safety Center, 1992.

Educated Public Relations: School Safety 101. Westlake Village, Calif.: National School Safety Center, 1986.

Erickson, F. "Conceptions of School Culture: An Overview," *Educational Administration Quarterly,* Vol. 23 (November, 1987).

Family Violence: Prevention and Treatment. Edited by Robert L. Hampton and others. Thousand Oaks, Calif.: Sage Publications, Inc., 1993.

Final Report: State Task Force on Gangs and Drugs. Sacramento: California Council on Criminal Justice, 1989.

Final Report: State Task Force on Youth Gang Violence. Sacramento: California Council on Criminal Justice, 1986.

Fingerhut, Lois A. "Firearm Mortality Among Children, Youth, and Young Adults 1–34 Years of Age, Trends and Current Status: United States, 1985–90," *Advance Data from Vital and Health Statistics,* Vol. 231 (March 23, 1993).

Freedom from Fear: Ending California's Hate Violence Epidemic. Final Report of the Lieutenant Governor's Commission on the Prevention of Hate Violence, January, 1993.

The Future by Design. A Community Framework: Preventing Alcohol and Other Drug Problems Through a Systems Approach. Washington, D.C.: U.S. Department of Health and Human Services, Center for Substance Abuse Prevention, 1991.

Gangs in Schools: Breaking Up Is Hard to Do. Westlake Village, Calif.: National School Safety Center, 1993.

Growing Up Drug Free: A Parent's Guide to Prevention. Washington, D.C.: U.S. Department of Education, 1990.

Journal of Emotional and Behavioral Problems: Reclaiming Children and Youth. Published by National Educational Service, Bloomington, Ind.

Kids in the Crossfire: An ABC Special with Peter Jennings. Taped at Eliot Junior High School, Washington, D.C. Broadcast in November, 1993.

LA Youth, The Newspaper by and About Los Angeles Teens, November-December, 1993.

Law in the School (Revised edition). Sacramento: Office of the California Attorney General, Crime and Violence Prevention Center, 1994.

Learning to Live Drug Free: A Curriculum Model for Prevention. Washington, D.C.: U.S. Department of Education, 1990.

The Need to Know: Juvenile Record Sharing. Westlake Village, Calif.: National School Safety Center, 1989.

Not Schools Alone: Guidelines for Schools and Communities to Prevent the Use of Tobacco, Alcohol, and Other Drugs Among Children and Youths. Sacramento: California Department of Education, 1991.

On Alert! Gang Prevention: School In-service Guidelines. Sacramento: California Department of Education, 1994.

Poplin, Mary, and Joseph Weers. *Voices from the Inside: A Report on Schooling from Inside the Classroom.* Claremont, Calif.: The Institute for Education in Transformation at The Claremont Graduate School, 1992.

Preventing Chaos in Times of Crisis: A Guide for School Administrators. Los Alamitos, Calif.: Southwest Regional Laboratory, 1992.

The Prevention of Youth Violence: A Framework for Community Action. Atlanta: National Center for Injury Prevention and Control, Centers for Disease Control and Prevention, 1993.

Prevention Plus II: Tools for Creating and Sustaining a Drug-Free Community. Washington, D.C.: U.S. Department of Health and Human Services, Center for Substance Abuse Prevention, 1989.

Prevention Plus III: Assessing Alcohol and Other Prevention Programs at the School and Community Level. Washington, D.C.: U.S. Department of Health and Human Services, Center for Substance Abuse Prevention, 1991.

Prevention Resource Guide: Elementary Youth. Washington, D.C.: U.S. Department of Health and Human Services, Center for Substance Abuse Prevention, 1991.

Prevention Resource Guide: Preschool Children. Washington, D.C.: U.S. Department of Health and Human Services, Center for Substance Abuse Prevention, 1990.

Prevention Resource Guide: Secondary School Students. Washington, D.C.: U.S. Department of Health and Human Services, Center for Substance Abuse Prevention, 1991.

"Project DARE: Teaching Kids to Say 'No' to Drugs and Alcohol," *Research in Action,* March, 1986. Newsletter published by the National Institute of Justice, U.S. Department of Justice, Washington, D.C.

School Attendance Improvement: A Blueprint for Action. Sacramento: California Department of Education, 1983.

School/Community Violence Prevention: Focus on Gangs. Sacramento: California Department of Education and Office of the California Attorney General, 1994.

School Crime. Washington, D.C.: U.S. Department of Justice, Bureau of Justice Statistics, 1991.

School Crime and Violence: Victim's Rights. Westlake Village, Calif.: National School Safety Center, 1992.

School Discipline Notebook (Revised edition). Westlake Village, Calif.: National School Safety Center, 1992.

School Safety Checkbook. Westlake Village, Calif.: National School Safety Center, 1990.

Schools and Drugs: A Guide to Drug and Alcohol Abuse Prevention Curricula and Programs (Revised edition). Sacramento: Office of the California Attorney General, Crime and Violence Prevention Center, 1991.

Set Straight on Bullies. Westlake Village, Calif.: National School Safety Center, 1989.

Suicide Prevention Program for California Public Schools. Sacramento: California Department of Education, 1987.

Prothrow-Stith, Deborah. *Deadly Consequences: How Violence Is Destroying Our Teenage Population and a Plan to Begin Solving the Problem.* New York: HarperCollins Publishers, 1993.

Toward a Drug-Free Generation: A Nation's Responsibility. Washington, D.C.: U.S. Department of Education and Office of National Drug Control Policy, 1990.

What Works: Schools Without Drugs. Washington, D.C.: U.S. Department of Education, 1992.

"When Killers Come to Class," *U.S. News & World Report,* November 8, 1993.

Youth Involvement: Developing Leaders and Strengthening Communities. Washington, D.C.: U.S. Department of Housing and Urban Development, Partners for Youth Leadership and the Office of Public and Indian Housing, 1990.

Videotapes

Chaos to Calm . . . Creating Safe Schools. Sacramento: Office of the California Attorney General, Crime and Violence Prevention Center, 1984.

Community-Oriented Policing and Problem Solving. Sacramento: Office of the California Attorney General, Crime and Violence Prevention Center, 1992 (video and guide).

Drug-Free Zones . . . Taking Action. Sacramento: Office of the California Attorney General, Crime and Violence Prevention Center, 1991.

Drugs and Youth . . . The Challenge (Revised). Sacramento: Office of the California Attorney General, Crime and Violence Prevention Center, 1991.

Gangs: Turning the Corner. Sacramento: Office of the California Attorney General, Crime and Violence Prevention Center, 1994.

High Risk Youth: At the Crossroads. Westlake Village, Calif.: National School Safety Center, 1989.

Raising Children in Troubled Times. Los Angeles: Los Angeles Unified School District, 1992. A video series to help parents deal successfully with the supervision and discipline of children; sets available in English or Spanish.

Safe Schools: A Guide for Action. Sacramento: Office of the California Attorney General, Crime and Violence Prevention Center, 1989.

School Crisis: Under Control. Westlake Village, Calif.: National School Safety Center, 1991.

Resource Centers

American Bar Association, Special Committee on Youth Education for Citizenship, 541 N. Fairbanks Ct., Chicago, IL 60611-3314; telephone (312) 988-5735

American Bar Association, Standing Committee on Dispute Resolution, 1800 M St., NW, Washington, DC 20036; telephone (202) 331-2258

California Attorney General, Crime and Violence Prevention Center, P. O. Box 944255, Sacramento, CA 94244-2550; telephone (916) 324-7863

California Department of Education, School Safety and Violence Prevention Office, P.O. Box 944272, Sacramento, CA 94244-2720; telephone (916) 657-2989

Center for Civic Education, 5146 Douglas Fir Rd., Calabasas, CA 91321; telephone (818) 591-9321

Center for Media Literacy, 1962 S. Shenandoah St., Los Angeles, CA 90034; telephone (310) 559-2944

Centers for Disease Control and Prevention, 255 East Paces Ferry Rd., Atlanta, GA 30305; telephone (404) 842-6796

Children's Safety Network, National Center for Education in Maternal and Child Health, 2000 15th St. North, Suite 701, Arlington, VA 22201-2617

Conflict Resolution Resources for Schools and Youths, Community Board Program, Inc., 1540 Market St., Suite 490, San Francisco, CA 94102-1250; telephone (415) 552-1250

Constitutional Rights Foundation, 407 S. Dearborn, Suite 1700, Chicago, IL 60605; telephone (312) 663-9057

Constitutional Rights Foundation, 601 S. Kingsley Dr., Los Angeles, CA 90005; telephone (213) 487-5590

Drug Information and Strategy Clearinghouse, P.O. Box 6424, Rockville, MD 20850; telephone (800) 955-2232

Drugs and Crime Data Center and Clearinghouse, 1600 Research Blvd., Rockville, MD 20850; telephone (800) 666-3332

National Association for Mediation in Education, 205 Hampshire House, P.O. Box 33635, University of Massachusetts, Amherst, MA 01003-3635; telephone (413) 545-2462

National Center for Health Statistics, 6525 Belcrest Rd., Hyattsville, MD 20782

National Clearinghouse for Alcohol and Drug Information, Box 2345, Rockville, MD 20852; telephone (800) 729-6686

National Criminal Justice Reference Service, Box 6000, Rockville, MD 20850; telephone (800) 851-3420

National Educational Service, 1610 W. Third St., P.O. Box 8, Bloomington, IN 47402; telephone (812) 336-7700

National Institute for Citizen Education in the Law, 711 G St., SE, Washington, DC 20003; telephone (202) 546-6644

National Institute for Dispute Resolution, 1901 L St., NW, Suite 600, Washington, DC 20036; telephone (202) 466-4764

National School Safety Center, 4165 Thousand Oaks Blvd., Suite 290, Westlake Village, CA 91362; telephone (805) 373-9977

U.S. Department of Education, Office of Elementary and Secondary Education, Drug Planning and Outreach Unit, 400 Maryland Ave., SW, Washington, DC 20202; telephone (800) 788-2800

Western Regional Center for Drug-Free Schools and Communities:

Northern California: Ralph F. Baker, Area Coordinator, Western Regional Center for Drug-Free Schools and Communities, Far West Laboratory, 730 Harrison St., San Francisco, CA 94107; telephone (415) 565-3000

Southern California: Carol F. Thomas, Area Coordinator, Western Regional Center for Drug-Free Schools and Communities, Southwest Regional Laboratory, 4665 Lampson Ave., Los Alamitos, CA 90720; telephone (310) 598-7661

Publications Available from the Department of Education

This publication is one of over 600 that are available from the California Department of Education. Some of the more recent publications or those most widely used are the following:

Item no.	Title (Date of publication)	Price
1372	Arts Work: A Call for Arts Education for All California Students: The Report of the Superintendent's Task Force on the Visual and Performing Arts (1997)	$11.25
1450	C.A.F.E.—Cafeteria Access for Everyone (video and guide) (1998)	14.00
1515	California Public School Directory, 2000	19.50
1498	California Safe Schools Assessment: 1998-99 Results (2000)	20.00
1492	California School Accounting Manual, 1999 Edition	25.00
0488	Caught in the Middle: Educational Reform for Young Adolescents in California Public Schools (1987)	9.25
1373	Challenge Standards for Student Success: Health Education (1998)	10.00
1409	Challenge Standards for Student Success: Language Arts Student Work Addendum (1998)	12.75
1435	Challenge Standards for Student Success: Physical Education (1998)	8.50
1429	Challenge Standards for Student Success: Visual and Performing Arts (1998)	12.50
1290	Challenge Toolkit: Family-School Compacts (1997)	9.75*
1439	Check It Out! Assessing School Library Media Programs: A Guide for School District Education Policy and Implementation Teams (1998)	9.25
1491	Collaborative Partners: California's Experience with the 1997 Head Start Expansion Grants (2000)	12.50
1391	Commodity Administrative Manual (1998)	19.50
1281	Connect, Compute, and Compete: The Report of the California Education Technology Task Force (1996)	5.75
1431	Early Identification/Early Intervention of Young Children with Emotional and Behavioral Issues: Trainer of Trainers Manual (1998)	30.00
1410	Ear-Resistible: Hearing Test Procedures for Infants, Toddlers, and Preschoolers, Birth Through Five Years of Age (1998)	10.00
1352	Educational Specifications: Linking Design of School Facilities to Educational Program (1997)	18.50
1476	Educating English Learners for the Twenty-First Century: The Report of the Proposition 227 Task Force (1999)	10.50
1509	Elementary Makes the Grade! (2000)	10.25
1389	English–Language Arts Content Standards for California Public Schools, Kindergarten Through Grade Twelve (1998)	9.25
1468	Enrolling Students Living in Homeless Situations (1999)	8.50
1244	Every Child a Reader: The Report of the California Reading Task Force (1995)	5.25
1475	First Class: A Guide for Early Primary Education (1999)	12.50
1388	First Look: Vision Evaluation and Assessment for Infants, Toddlers, and Preschoolers, Birth Through Five Years of Age (1998)	10.00
0804	Foreign Language Framework for California Public Schools, Kindergarten Through Grade Twelve (1989)	7.25
1355	The Form of Reform: School Facility Design Implications for California Educational Reform (1997)	18.50
1378	Fostering the Development of a First and a Second Language in Early Childhood: Resource Guide (1998)	10.75
1382	Getting Results, Part I: California Action Guide to Creating Safe and Drug-Free Schools and Communities (1998)	15.25
1493	Getting Results, Part II: California Action Guide to Tobacco Use Prevention Education (2000)	13.50
1482	Getting Results, Update 1, Positive Youth Development: Research, Commentary, and Action (1999)	12.00
1408	Guide and Criteria for Program Quality Review: Elementary Grades (1998)	13.50
1268	Guidelines for Occupational Therapy and Physical Therapy in California Public Schools (1996)	12.50
1465	Handbook on Administration of Early Childhood Special Education Programs (2000)	13.50
1463	Handbook on Assessment and Evaluation in Early Childhood Special Education Programs (2000)	13.50
1464	Handbook on Family Involvement in Early Childhood Special Education Programs (1999)	11.25
1380	Health Careers Education 2000: A Program Guide (1998)	20.00
1064	Health Framework for California Public Schools, Kindergarten Through Grade Twelve (1994)	10.00
1477	Helping Your Students with Homework (1999)	9.25
0737	Here They Come: Ready or Not—Report of the School Readiness Task Force (summary report) (1988)	5.00
1488	History–Social Science Content Standards for California Public Schools, Kindergarten Through Grade Twelve (2000)	9.00
1284	History–Social Science Framework for California Public Schools, 1997 Updated Edition (1997)	12.50
1245	Improving Mathematics Achievement for All California Students: The Report of the California Mathematics Task Force (1995)	5.25

* Other titles in the *Challenge Toolkit* series are *Outline for Assessment and Accountability Plans* (item no. 1300), *Safe and Healthy Schools* (item no. 1299), *School Facilities* (item no. 1294), *Site-Based Decision Making* (item no. 1295), *Service-Learning* (item no. 1291), *Student Activities* (item no. 1292), and *Student Learning Plans* (item no. 1296). Call 1-800-995-4099 for prices and shipping charges.

Prices and availability are subject to change without notice. Please call 1-800-995-4099 for current prices and shipping charges.

1500	Independent Study Operations Manual (2000 Edition)	$30.00
1024	It's Elementary! Elementary Grades Task Force Report (1992)	9.00
1442	Joining Hands: Preparing Teachers to Make Meaningful Home-School Connections (1998)	13.25
1252	Just Kids: A Training Manual for Working with Children Prenatally Substance-Exposed (1996)	22.25
1457	Mathematics Content Standards for California Public Schools, Kindergarten Through Grade Twelve (1999)	8.50
1508	Mathematics Framework for California Public Schools, Kindergarten Through Grade Twelve (2000 Revised Edition)	17.50
1213	Model Program Standards for Adult Basic Education (1996)	11.50
1248	Model Program Standards for Adult Secondary Education (1996)	11.50
1384	Observing Preschoolers: Assessing First and Second Language Development (video) (1998)	12.00
1065	Physical Education Framework for California Public Schools, Kindergarten Through Grade Twelve (1994)	7.75
1314	Positive Intervention for Serious Behavior Problems: Best Practices in Implementing the Hughes Bill (Assembly Bill 2586) and the Positive Behavioral Intervention Regulations (1998)	14.00
1289	Program Guidelines for Students Who Are Visually Impaired, 1997 Revised Edition	10.00
1502	Programs for Deaf and Hard of Hearing Students: Guidelines for Quality Standards (2000)	12.00
1462	Reading/Language Arts Framework for California Public Schools, Kindergarten Through Grade Twelve (1999)	17.50
1399	Ready to Learn—Quality Preschools for California in the 21st Century: The Report of the Superintendent's Universal Preschool Task Force (1998)	8.00
1171	Recommended Readings in Literature, Kindergarten Through Grade Eight, Revised Annotated Edition (1996)	10.00
1315	Reducing Exceptional Stress and Trauma: Curriculum and Intervention Guidelines (1997)	17.00
1316	Reducing Exceptional Stress and Trauma: Facilitator's Guide (1997)	18.00
1318	Room at the Table: Meeting Children's Special Needs at Mealtimes (video and guide) (1997)	17.00
1191	Safe Schools: A Planning Guide for Action (1995 Edition)	11.00
1496	Science Content Standards for California Public Schools, Kindergarten Through Grade Twelve (2000)	9.00
0870	Science Framework for California Public Schools, Kindergarten Through Grade Twelve (1990)	9.50
1445	Science Safety Handbook for California Public Schools (1999 Edition)	17.50
1387	School District Organization Handbook (1998)	24.50
1411	School Nutrition Programs Guidance Manual (1998)	30.00
1402	School Safety—Addendum to Safe Schools: A Planning Guide for Action (1998)	8.25
1452	Service-Learning: Linking Classrooms and Communities: The Report of the Superintendent's Service Learning Task Force (1999)	7.00
1407	Steering by Results—A High-Stakes Rewards and Interventions Program for California Schools and Students: The Report of the Rewards and Interventions Advisory Committee (1998)	8.00
1472	Strategic Teaching and Learning: Standards-Based Instruction to Promote Content Literacy in Grades Four Through Twelve (2000)	12.50
1277	Strategies for Success: A Resource Manual for SHAPE (Shaping Health as Partners in Education) (1996)	15.00
1383	Talking with Preschoolers: Strategies for Promoting First and Second Language Development (video) (1998)	12.00
1255	Taking Charge: A Disaster Preparedness Guide for Child Care and Development Centers (1996)	10.25
1261	Visual and Performing Arts Framework for California Public Schools, Kindergarten Through Grade Twelve (1996)	15.00
1392	Work-Based Learning Guide (1998)	12.50
1390	Work Permit Handbook for California Schools (1998)	13.00
1381	Workforce Career Development Model (1998)	9.50

Orders should be directed to:

California Department of Education
CDE Press, Sales Office
P.O. Box 271
Sacramento, CA 95812-0271

Please include the item number and desired quantity for each title ordered. Shipping and handling charges are additional, and purchasers in California also add county sales tax.

Mail orders must be accompanied by a check, a purchase order, or a credit card number, including expiration date (VISA or MasterCard only). Purchase orders without checks are accepted from educational institutions, businesses, and governmental agencies. Telephone orders will be accepted toll-free (1-800-995-4099) for credit card purchases. *All sales are final.*

The *Educational Resources Catalog* contains illustrated, annotated listings of departmental publications, videos, and other instructional materials. Free copies of the *Catalog* may be obtained by writing to the address given above or by calling (916) 445-1260.

Prices and availability are subject to change without notice. Please call 1-800-995-4099 for current prices and shipping charges.

R99-084 002-1224-208 7-00 2M